Please return to:
The Library
Senior Center of West Seattle
4217 SW Oregon St.
Seattle, WA 98116

PICTURES, MOVING

A SHORT STORY COLLECTION

BY

JAMES THOMAS

DRAGON GATE, INC.

PORT TOWNSEND, WASHINGTON

The stories in this collection originally appeared in the following publica-
tions: "Last Factory Blues" in *The Smith*; "Half Frame" in *Intro 12*; "Christ-
mas in Calpe" in *Chariton Review*; "Santorini Gray" in *Mississippi Review*;
"Paco and I at Sea" in *Esquire*; "Barbecue" in *Carolina Quarterly*; "Blood
Money" in *Quarterly West*; and "Talma Levy Is Falling" in the *Cimarron
Review*.

The author is especially grateful for the time and opportunities provided
by a Wallace Stegner Writing Fellowship from Stanford University (1977-
78), a James Michener Award from the Iowa Writers' Workshop (1981-82),
and a grant from the National Endowment for the Arts (1983).

The publisher and author thank the National Endowment for the Arts
for a grant that helped support the publication of this book.

Published by Dragon Gate, Inc.
508 Lincoln Street, Port Townsend, WA 98368

LIBRARY OF CONGRESS CATALOGING IN PUBLICATION DATA

THOMAS, JAMES, 1946-
    PICTURES, MOVING.

    CONTENTS: HALF FRAME — SPARKLE IN FIVE —
SANTORINI GRAY — [ETC.]
    I. TITLE.
PS3570.H564P5   1985   813'.   85-4334
ISBN 0-937872-22-9
ISBN 0-937872-23-7 (PBK.)

Contents

PICTURES, MOVING

∘
∘   ∘
∘

° °
° °
°

Half Frame

Our souls are like those orphans whose unwedded
mothers die in bearing them: the secret of our paternity
lies in the grave, and we must there learn it.

> — Herman Melville,
> from "The Gilder"
> in *Moby Dick*

GARRETT IS STANDING on the deck of the boat, at the
rail, looking out. The sky and the sea are welded together
now, made of precisely the same slate gray, and above the
watery seam the sun and the moon are both faintly visible:
two dull disks of white. It is a ghostly double exposure. With
his hand, Garrett shutters his eyes.

Behind his hand, Garrett stands at the door of the barn,
at the gate, looking up. The Greek's bulging eyes do not
blink, his bloodless lips do not move. Garrett stares at Alexis
and Alexis stares back. Between the two men, the nervous
horses paw the ground. It is getting dark — darker still in the
barn — but it is a long moment before Garrett can look away,
can drop his fingers and release the image of the man suspended in the dry, dusty air.

3

Along with the last light of the Athenian day, the rain is still falling on the port of Piræus. It has rained all day, but now the moisture falling from above seems to have no more substance than that blown up by the wind from the sea below. The *Naxos* is about to put to sea.

Two Greeks in blue navy pea coats with turned-up collars and blue woolen caps are letting out the long, slow lines, the gray hawsers that have held the *Naxos* to its berth all day. They are late; the boat is late; across the deck they shout urgent, belated instructions at one another.

The *Naxos* is twelve hours behind schedule. The difference between the day's first light and its last, thinks Garrett, no difference at all.

Beneath the deck, which rattles and shakes, he can hear and feel the powerful engines, pulling at the line, tearing at the water. But they have not left yet; the line attests to that. On the dock, half a hundred people watch the boat's uncertain progress as it tries to back away. Lex's sister is among them.

Then Garrett hears the gulls and looks up. Above the boat they scream and turn, then climb the gray sky only to fall forward, like clumsy acrobats

o

Before Garrett discovers Alexis in the barn, and long before Athens, Piræus, and the *Naxos*, Garrett and Lex live together, share the rent on an old farmhouse situated among the fields and factories of Ohio. It is late spring and wet, a brown and muddy inland world.

Neither of them is a farmer. Garrett works in town, at the county hospital, where he helps fix broken bones: bones broken by fallen trees and slammed car doors, on wet or icy streets, bones broken on dark nights, in fights and motorcycle spills, and because of old age. Garrett is the cast man.

Each day, in a little room off the main corridor of the orthopedics ward, he mixes plaster, lays out gauze bandage, makes sure the saw is sharp. He does not much care for his work.

4

Alexis has lived at the farmhouse now for three months, ever since Trish moved out. He is a chemist at the University, a Greek graduate student who loves his work. Garrett learned these things the day Lex moved in, the day he answered Garrett's ad in the local paper. Garrett doesn't know much more about him now.

Alexis is not a talker. Early each morning Garrett finds him in the living room, cross-legged on the living room couch, reading the *Toledo Blade*. He takes a full hour over the news, without drink, without food, without getting up or changing position. His expression over what he reads ranges from disapproval to disgust. Occasionally he lets out a small damning groan. But he does not talk.

They have sometimes spoken a little in the evening, before Alexis returns to his lab at the University, where he works late. It is unnerving for Garrett, having this silent Greek in the house where he lived for so long with Trish. Instead of replacing her ghost, as he had hoped, it seems to Garrett that he now lives with two of them.

o

It takes Garrett nearly a year to save the money, but when he goes, he goes directly; flies from Toledo to New York, and from there straight to Athens.

His first three days in the Greek capital are a disappointment. Athens is nothing like what he expected. It is noisy and dirty and congested, an architectural wasteland of sooty concrete inhabited by people who seem to have lost their vision. It smells of neglect.

Nonetheless, using Lex's camera, Garrett takes pictures. Of the Acropolis, overrun by disappointed tourists like himself; of the soiled but still-standing Parthenon; the squalid marketplace; the late afternoon crush of Greeks in Omonia Square.

He tries to take the photographs the way Lex would have, carefully composing each frame.

On the fourth day he finds Lex's sister at the Griva Travel

5

Agency where she works, the address of which Lex had left for him — on the box that was to contain the photo album. Instead he has brought the photo album to give her in person. And he has brought his questions.

But before he can ask them she has talked him into a boat ticket, the *Naxos*, an island cruise.

"You have come the perfect time of year," she says. "Before it is hot and before all the Germans. And the islands are most beautiful in the spring. The rain will not last."

Garrett agrees to buy the ticket, and when she offers to accompany him to the port of Piræus — this friend of her brother's — Garrett agrees to that also. Perhaps, he thinks, he can ask his questions then.

o

It is the wettest spring in forty years according to McPherson, Garrett's ancient landlord who owns half of Portage County.

McPherson doesn't so much farm his land as mine it, getting exponentially richer each year from his corn and beans and from his tenants. Each month he comes around in person to see Garrett, to check on the buildings, collect the rent, shoot the country breeze. Each month he leans in the doorway, chews on an Ohio Blue Tip match, trembles and bitches.

And this month he has more than the weather and the rent on his mind.

"That Arab has got to go," he says after a minute. "I been thinking about it and I shouldn't have let you bring in somebody without me knowing who it was first. They've been talking about him all over the county and I don't want my name mixed up in it."

"What is it they've been saying, Mr. McPherson?" Garrett has already handed over the envelope containing the two checks.

"Just that I got one on my land and it's bad business. You know what they're doing with that oil money. Buying up banks and hotels everyplace, and farms. I read in the paper that they've been buying up farms in Iowa. Ohio could be next."

"He doesn't have that kind of money, Mr. McPherson. He's just a poor graduate student at the University. And he's a Greek, not an Arab."

"Look boy, don't go twisting things around. I've seen him. I want him out of here by next month. You should never have let that woman of yours go, and now we'll just have to find somebody else if you can't live alone. Understand?"

"Sure, Mr. McPherson, I understand. I'll talk to him about it."

Garrett knows as he speaks that he will not talk to Alexis about it. Not that he wouldn't be happy enough if the Greek left the farm. He simply doesn't like the old man's motives, or his tactics — if he wants Alexis out, he'll have to do the dirty work himself.

It has occurred to Garrett many times, ever since Trish left, that perhaps *he* should leave the farm; but he knows that he won't, not yet. He likes the openness of the fields around him and the creek that wanders through them like a crooked smile; he likes the outbuildings behind the house and especially the old barn, rented to a neighbor whose horses, which he keeps there, are ignored for days at a time; he likes the huge pine tree that stands in front of the house and towers over it in permanent green both summer and winter; he even likes the small country cemetery, on the low hill across the road, at which he has seen McPherson nervously glance.

He does not want to give these things up, not yet, nor is he willing to pass McPherson's unkind sentiments on to Lex, who has, just in the past week, become slightly less reclusive. The Greek has even begun to talk a little, not about chemistry but about his newly acquired interest. Lex has, suddenly, become passionate about photography.

"I want to make a record of everything," he explains to Garrett. "I want my sister to see where I have been. I want

7

her to understand why I am doing what I am doing."

Lex's sister lives in Greece. In Athens. She is his only family, Garrett learns to his surprise, having imagined a multitude of siblings in some small Greek village. She works at a travel agency and has no children at all.

At first the photographs are simple snapshots, taken with the Instamatic that Lex has apparently had for years. Each day he brings home a new packet of developed prints, which he shyly insists Garrett look at.

The first stack is of Lex's lab at school, long counters cluttered with glass and plastic tubing and stainless steel dishes, serious young men bent over clipboards and digital computers, long and complicated formulas covering a blackboard. The next day the pictures are all of the University campus, of students hurrying between classes, shots of older buildings, the square windowless library, the botanical gardens, the huge rocks cemented to the ground in front of the Geology building. The pictures are amateurish but carefully composed, impersonal as the photographs of property taken by insurance companies.

The third day the prints are drab, of town: shop fronts, traffic at stoplights, housewives and farmers and businessmen frozen to the sidewalks.

"I am learning," says Alexis. "Photography is not so easy like people think."

After a week he abandons his Instamatic, buys a much more expensive 35 mm Nikon with three lenses and tripod, and a Sony microcassette tape recorder which he surely cannot afford. He starts over. With the ten-second self-timer on the new camera, he can now get himself into the picture.

New photographs of the lab include himself in white jacket. In sport coat and tie, he stands — a young professional — before the University buildings. With packages under his arms, he poses with a parking meter in front of Wigdahl's Hardware Store downtown.

And on tape now there are sounds to go with the pictures: lab noises and lab talk, students gossiping in the Student

Union, the horns and screeching tires of traffic on the street, rock music, cash registers registering, people laughing, clowning, coughing.

But the sounds are so random and disconnected that Garrett can make little sense of them; and when Lex's voice comes on, as though to explain a scene, it is in garbled, unintelligible Greek. Garrett begins to lose interest.

"I suppose," says Lex, "that I will have to edit them. Even for my sister."

One morning Garrett discovers that it has stopped raining, and after work that evening he begins to plant a garden. The ground is really still too damp, but it is already June, absurdly late in the season, and it is now or never. He plants peas that should have gone into the ground a month ago, cheats by putting in tomato and pepper plants that are already twelve inches high, lays down a row of carrots out of a sense of tradition rather than taste. He hates carrots.

When it gets dark he showers with satisfaction. It feels good to have gotten so dirty, done something with a future.

Garrett's dwindling interest in Lex's photography is returned by Lex's apparent interest in Garrett's garden. The next evening the Greek gets back to the farm before dark, sets up his tripod, and begins taking pictures.

Garrett is busy with seeds for lettuce and cucumbers, beans and summer squash. There is not much to photograph; the garden really only exists beneath the earth and in the imagination, but Lex shoots a full roll of film anyway. Garrett is largely indifferent. He does not want to be distracted from this new beginning, this hard work in the dirt, but he nonetheless allows Lex to set up his camera one more time and they pose together for several shots: Garrett with a hoe in his hand and a silly grin on his face and Alexis, in new cashmere sweater and penny loafers he is careful not to soil, standing above and beside Garrett like a Greek gentleman farmer. Garrett thinks he would like to slip one of these pictures into the envelope with the rent checks when McPherson comes around the first of next month.

Garrett and Alexis do not exactly become friends, but with Lex's new openness they establish a kind of rapport composed of tolerance and respect, and the farm, for Garrett, once again begins to feel like home. Lex is more often there in the evenings now — sorting photographs, arranging them in the several leather-bound albums he has bought, speaking Greek into his tape recorder — and Garrett does not mind.

Garrett even begins to feel a certain fraternal concern for Alexis. For one thing he wonders about the money this new hobby, not to mention the new clothes, must be costing.

"Not to worry," says Lex, examining no fewer than twenty photographs of the Wood County Courthouse, a huge orange building of gables and spires. "It is what I have saved out of my grant this year; before I was foolishly frugal."

"What about the time? I thought you had a lot of work at your lab."

"It is not so important as I thought. Did you know," he says, "that on the third floor of this courthouse there is a little museum, and in it there is a human thumb in a bottle?" He reaches for another stack of photos, all of the museum, and shows Garrett the picture of the bottle and the thumb. "I don't know whose it is," he says.

His photographs are, at least, getting better. The lighting is right, often interesting, the subject matter is more carefully considered, more artfully framed. From each pile of prints, Lex selects only a few to go into the albums.

"Tomorrow," he says, "I am taking the day off to do nothing but shoot the farm. Will you be here?"

The next day is Saturday. Garrett is there, shows Lex some of the less obvious features of the buildings and property, watches as the Greek shoots half a roll of film on the neighbor's horses, walks with him up and down the creek, which is more shallow now. On Sunday Lex goes alone to Toledo, to photograph the airport he says, the first place he ever walked on American soil.

On Monday Garrett helps set hips and ankles and arms, ribs and wrists and knees. It is a never-ending procession of broken bodies, Demerol-dulled patients and chatty doctors, but through it all he cannot get Lex off his mind. Never before, not even with Trish, who became pathologically neat during the month before she left the farm, has he known anyone to become so easily obsessed with something so recently unfamiliar. Not that such things are necessarily bad. In Trish's case, of course, it was a symptom of a deeper dissatisfaction, but with Alexis it seems just the opposite. His solid contentment and newfound good humor are beginning to infect even Garrett. But he is puzzled.

The doctors note Garrett's distraction, interpret it wrongly, tell him he needs to go out after work and get plastered. Garrett grimaces at their little pun, tells them to give him a break, gets on with his job.

What he cannot understand is the ease with which Alexis seems to have arrived at new happiness in his life through something as simple as photography. Garrett glances at the X-ray lit up on the wall viewer, life clearly exposed on the inside and in this case shattered, and wonders.

A few days later, when the school quarter is over, Lex takes an entire week off from the lab and devotes himself entirely to his camera and tape recorder.

He experiments with slides but goes back to prints, talks about setting up a darkroom in the basement, talks about how he could get most of the chemicals for nothing, but in the end decides it would take too much time. Stacks of photos, of everything, appear everywhere. Garrett watches with more and more interest as the piles mount, amazed at the Greek's outpour of energy, his almost adolescent enthusiasm. More than once Garrett has seen him smile at nothing.

Garrett works in his garden. Faint lines of green — carrots and peas and lettuce — appear on the face of the earth.

Alexis buys two more photo albums, fills them. Late at night Garrett can hear him, in his room, dictating into his tape recorder. Garrett begins to wish that he could understand the language so that he might know what Lex is talking about, across time, to his sister, in Athens.

June creeps on. It finally turns hot. If there is a breeze, it blows hardest on the hill across the road, through the cemetery, and at sunset Garrett often walks there. One evening Lex joins him.

"It's a pleasant place this time of day," says Garrett. "Trish and I used to come here a lot. Then she said she didn't have time, had to clean the house."

"I haven't photographed it," says Alexis, "but it's perfect. Just what I need." He pushes with his penny loafers at a headstone that has fallen over, tries to right it but cannot. "I will shoot it tomorrow," he says, "at exactly this time. When the light is right."

When Lex's week of vacation is up, he does not go back to work at the lab. "I need a little more time," he says, "then I'll be done. Then it won't matter. They can fire me if they want."

The photographs of the cemetery turn out nicely, the fallen red sun lending a rose patina to the white stones. The green grass combed by the late afternoon breeze, and the fields stretching with new life toward the horizon, provide a perfect backdrop. In half the shots, Lex has framed himself, center and forward; in the rest, he is turned away from the camera, his hands on his hips as though surveying, from a firm position over the dead, his world, distance, eternity.

"It is almost done," he says. "Now I have only to put together the finished product." All night Garrett hears the Greek talking, in his room; but in the morning Garrett is surprised to find Lex on the living room floor, disassembling his four photo albums, until he realizes that they are all being consolidated into one. "I am making decisions," says the Greek, "hard choices. I have not slept. It is not easy."

Garrett goes to work. He helps to pin a hip in the morning and spends the afternoon removing casts, an easy day. When he gets home the house is quiet. Lex's motorcycle is in the driveway, the air conditioner in the living room has been turned on, there are no more photos stacked on chairs and end tables. Lex's bedroom door is shut. Finished, thinks Garrett, done. Sleeping. And wonders if things will be different now, if Lex will once again become withdrawn, quiet, private.

Garrett fools around in the garden, takes a short turn through the cemetery, then – when Lex is still not up – changes clothes and for the first time in weeks goes into town for a beer. Were the Greek awake, Garrett would have invited him along. But when he gets home, after one in the morning, the house is still quiet. Lex's door is still shut. Garrett puts himself to bed.

The next day the hospital air conditioning breaks down, a child they are afraid to anesthetize is brought in screaming with a pulverized tibia, and Garrett has to stay late when the cast man on the late shift doesn't show up until after six. Through it all Garrett is exhausted from having stayed out too late the night before, and when he goes home it is with a headache, soaked in perspiration and saturated with ill humor, ready for aspirin and a very early night. And although he has, of course, been curious about Lex, he is in fact glad when he does not meet the Greek at the door, in the kitchen, in the living room. The bedroom door is still shut.

Garrett fixes himself a tuna fish sandwich and sits down in front of the television. When there is a commercial he shuts his eyes. When he thinks he hears a noise from Lex's room, he opens them. The news is over. Compulsively he goes to the Greek's bedroom door, stands by it a moment and then when he hears nothing, opens it. Alexis is not there.

Now Garrett is awake. He decides that a number of things are possible, the most likely of which is that Lex is off with friends, probably from the lab, who picked him up at the farm. Still, he is uneasy. Outside it is still light. With his unfinished sandwich in his hand, he lets the screen door slam behind him and stands in the driveway above the garden. It needs weeding for the first time.

Behind the house he discovers small hard apples on the apple trees, pears on the pear trees. He can see no evidence of cherries.

He decides to visit the horses. He has brought nothing for them to eat — even his sandwich is finished now — but they greet him anyway with great whinnies of expectation. Garrett reaches across the gate of the big barn to stroke one of them on the head, the flat-faced mare that is his favorite. She strikes her right foot at the ground and throws back her head. Garrett regrets again that he has brought nothing for her. She seems agitated, angry. He apologizes aloud, soothingly, and again reaches out. The mare backs off, hesitantly it seems to Garrett, into the barn. He follows her with his eyes. She does not go far, six feet perhaps, but far enough for Garrett to identify the source of her agitation. Hanging from the rafters by a rope, well off the ground in the dark dusty air, is Alexis.

For a long time Garrett is aware only of the noise of the horses, all three of them making low nervous sounds that shatter the evening, and the lifeless shape suspended behind and above them. Then, slowly, without thinking, Garrett allows his eyes to work with details. The thick dust filtering through the air in the last slanting light, the dark puffiness of the Greek's face, the ancient slats of the corral below; and the camera, behind the gate at the back of the building, posed effeminately on the telescoped legs of the tripod, more alive in its delicate spiderlike form than the man whose last breathing image it had unquestionably recorded. How, wonders Garrett, did he intend to get that last photograph into his album?

The answer makes Garrett swallow the saliva that has been accumulating in his mouth. The Greek's eyes stare pleadingly from their sockets.

o

Alexis's sister has come with him to the port of Piræus, and when they learn that the *Naxos* will be late, she sits with him in a cheerless café where they drink black, chewy coffee out of tiny cups, watch the rain fall, and talk.

She is, he guesses, thirty years old; and he learns that she has once, for two weeks, been to New York. She does not know what to think about America. Garrett says he does not yet know what to make of Greece.

It takes him a long time to work up to his questions, which he has carried for a year and now this long distance; questions which in the end have settled, like the thick grounds in his empty coffee cup, into a single dark substance.

"Why," he asks, "would your brother do such a thing?"

And he sees in her face, as he asks it, that she is anxious for him to leave — or the rain to let up and for the *Naxos* to depart.

"Why should anyone do such a thing?" she says. "And why do you ask me? I knew him only a long time ago. You say you lived with him. If anyone should know, it would be you."

"Yes," says Garrett, staring into his cup. The way she speaks reminds him of Trish. "But I don't. I don't know."

"Then you must stop thinking of it," she says sadly. "For your own good."

o

Garrett stares at Alexis and Alexis stares back. The horses paw at the ground. Garrett stands at the barn door, unable to move, unable to wipe the sweat from his forehead or blow away the flies that walk across his upper lip; stands frozen to the dying moment until he finds himself moving around the barn, outside, to the back, where he takes the camera from the tripod, tears from it the roll of film, and hurls it in the half-light of dusk over McPherson's green field, end over end toward the creek; then moves slowly to the house where he will wait for someone to come, for sirens, lights, the aftermath of an accident, the white stretcher and sheet; to the house where he will find himself sitting through the night, waiting for morning, first light, sleep.

o

15

Gulls climb in the sky: dull white forms, flapping and turning on gray. Then another boat, farther out in the harbor, lets out a long, deep-throated blast of its foghorn, thickening the air. It is a calling home, a calling away, and like a younger brother who has been left behind, the *Naxos* responds with a slip of its engine; and somewhere above, in the smoky steerage cabin, a chin-high lever is pulled by a man Garrett imagines in neat blue jacket with white braid trim, a blue-visored cap, and gloves.

The lines are thrown from shore to deck, the echo of the foghorn sinks beneath the water, and the *Naxos*, released from all constraints, leans heavily into the sea.

Like a tiny piece of dry ice sizzling in its own steam, the timeless moment evaporates and is gone.

Now comes the blink, the aftermath of the moment, the living negative that appears behind the eyelids after the bright flash. The blacks and whites of the perfect photograph are reversed. In the awkward image, Garrett sees himself waving. Below, on the pier, Lex's sister turns to leave.

And Garrett thinks: every man should be seen off, every man should have a friend. Every kindness ever shown should be repaid.

The sky darkens, the sun slips away. The *Naxos*, with its hawsers coiled on the deck like great fat snakes and the gulls following above, has started to pitch and roll.

The pier, in the distance now, has become a miniature with small unreal figures moving about on it. And it has become colder.

Garrett stands at the rail and watches. Behind the pier the lights of Piræus, and behind Piræus the yellow lights of Athens, are flickering through the haze. They could be stars. And somewhere in it, behind one of those hills, Garrett imagines the Acropolis as a floodlit postcard, mist drifting up through the columns of the Parthenon, the image perfectly framed, a photographer's dream.

Sparkle in Five

SHE WAS EIGHTEEN, he was thirty-nine. Still, there was heat. Fire.

In the beginning Fogarty had been surprised to notice *her* watching *him*, as he moved shirtlessly in and out of the Newgate Apartments to paint empty units, replace broken glass, fix hopeless plumbing. That was in early June. That was when he began to watch back.

She wore, always it seemed, white shorts and a halter top. Only the color of the top changed. Long dark hair flew around her bare brown shoulders. June, and she was already tan. And her door, apartment number five, was always open; so that whenever Fogarty entered the Newgate there she was, perfectly framed for him on her couch at the end of the dark dusty hall, watching television or reading a romance magazine.

He could not say now just when it was he had begun to let his interest in her show openly; but more and more often that month he hesitated at her door, with a comment about the weather or the state of the world, with a request for the time or a glass of cold water. And still he never expected anything more than the usual pleasantries, common tenant courtesy, in return.

Then they had come unexpectedly together, made love late one afternoon after she offered him a cold beer instead of water, pulled him into her apartment with her crooked smile and the fan turned on high. It had not mattered then that the couch was lumpy and full of erupting springs. But now things were complicated.

Her name was Sparkle. That's what she had written, in flowery blue Magic Marker, on her mailbox. No last name. After they had made love that first time, he had asked her what her name really was. Under duress — Fogarty literally, if playfully, pinning her small body down on the couch — she had admitted another. But the next day he discovered he had already forgotten it, and in his chagrin he had never been able to ask her again.

Things were now complicated because her rent was due, more than due, nearly two months late. August was nearly over. Jackson, the Newgate's owner and Fogarty's boss, was already concerned; and now Fogarty, as Jackson's employee, found himself sweating and miserable at Sparkle's open door. In his role as apartment manager he did not feel welcome over the threshold.

"Look," he was saying, "you know I don't personally give a damn, but Jackson is going to have my ass if you don't come up with something soon."

"I couldn't come up with cross-town bus fare at the moment," she said. She was sitting cross-legged on her couch next to a newly surfaced spring. "You know that."

"He's talking about eviction," said Fogarty. This wasn't exactly true, but it was bound to come up sooner or later; probably sooner. "He's talking about throwing you out."

"No, he can't," said Sparkle. "I have a complaint. My toilet doesn't work. I don't have to pay rent when my toilet doesn't work. I have to use the one in that empty apartment, you know, the one you just painted."

Sparkle's malfunctioning toilet was not news. A week before water had begun to leak from beneath the bowl, at the foot of the fixture, into the green shag carpet, which was now sodden. He had tried to fix it and failed.

"Then you do have the money," he said slowly, tentatively, "and simply refuse to pay, right?"

"Wrong. I don't have the money but I still refuse to pay."

Fogarty sighed. "Look, Spark," he said, "Jackson's not going to fix your toilet *until* you pay. You're two months late. That only makes sense."

"No, it doesn't. And besides, how can I pay when I'm not getting paid?"

"Wait a minute," he said, holding up his hand, "it's not Jackson's fault you lost your job."

"Do you think it was mine?" Sparkle put on her pout.

She had already told him the story: how her boss at the warehouse where she worked nights had gotten a little too friendly with his hands, and she had rashly reacted with a knee to his groin. She had been asked to pick up her check the next morning – and, Fogarty figured, no doubt had spent it by noon.

"Then borrow," he said. "Borrow from somebody if you have to."

"Who?"

"Your parents? Or one of your friends; you seem to have a lot of friends." Lately Fogarty had observed a regular parade of people circulating through the building, in and out of her apartment.

"My friends don't have any money – and my folks won't even talk to me on the phone right now. I've told you that."

"Then your brother." He had seen and met her brother, a large rough-looking kid of maybe twenty-five who often visited her, pulling his big and obviously expensive motorcycle inside the front hall of the Newgate.

"He got in an accident."

"On his bike?"

"With a car."

Fogarty pictured the collision. Twisted metal and body parts, blood on the pavement, pain. It made him grimace. "Was he hurt bad?"

"Not bad," said Sparkle. "He was arrested."

"Arrested? Why?"

"It was a stolen car."

Now Fogarty was confused. "He ran into a stolen car?"

"No. He was driving a stolen car."

Fogarty tried to find the motorcycle in the changing picture; couldn't. "Then what was the accident?" he asked helplessly.

"*That* was the accident," she said. "He was driving a stolen car and got stopped, accidentally, because the taillights didn't work. It was an *accident* that he got arrested."

Then Sparkle's face, which had until now been full of its usual playfulness, abruptly collapsed.

"He'll probably have to go back to prison," she said.

o

The next afternoon Jackson came by. Fogarty, standing at his front window, from which he could observe the Newgate across the street and watch the neighborhood, saw the white Jaguar pull up.

Fogarty waited for the phone to ring. In the back seat of the car he could see two of Jackson's kids, small girls, slapping at each other.

The phone rang. Fogarty answered it. It was Jackson.

"I'm out front," he said.

"I can see you," said Fogarty. "Nice wax job."

"Father's Day present. It was all my kids could afford. A wax job. I was hoping for maybe a new pair of shoes."

"Makes the car look like a million bucks." Fogarty could see the phone in Jackson's right hand.

"I wish. I could use a million bucks." Fogarty watched him mouth the words into the receiver. "But the truth is I don't own a tire of it, my check to the state for the plates is going to bounce, and I can't fill it with gas. It's all a front. Nobody will buy property from a man who doesn't appear to be doing well himself. What's our situation across the street, shall I come in?"

"I'll come out. I've got money for you." A minute later, bank bag in hand, Fogarty was standing beside the car. Jackson rolled down his window only halfway, obviously reluctant to let in the foul city air. The two little girls in back were arguing loudly over who got to play with a micro-cassette tape recorder.

"I've got to drop them off at the dentist," explained Jackson, trying to quiet them. They ignored him. "The other three need to go just as bad, but this is all my credit will stand. What have you got?"

"A hundred and eighty from number seven," said Fogarty, making the cash deposit through the half-open window, "which should at least fill your tank and a couple of teeth, and a solid promise from the people in nine who are sixty short. For tomorrow. I'll give you a call. Number two is empty and painted. I put out the sign."

"What about five?" asked Jackson. "That girl?"

Fogarty studied the silk handkerchief that bloomed from the breast pocket of Jackson's white summer suit.

"We may have a plumbing problem there," he said.

"She's the one who's nearly two months behind, isn't she?"

"Right. It's the toilet, leaks at the base. I couldn't fix it. We'll probably have to call a real plumber."

"How long has it been broken?"

"A week."

"Two months at one-ninety is three-eighty. I think we have to do something."

"She says she won't pay until it's fixed."

"How can I pay for a plumber?"

"She lost her job."

"And I'm getting calls from three banks and my health insurance company. Nobody works for himself anymore. What can I do?" Jackson sniffed hard, rubbed at his nose with his finger, but did not reach for his handkerchief. "Look," he said, "let's give her until Friday. This is Tuesday. It has to be in writing. Three days. State law. You have to tack a notice to her door. Okay?"

Fogarty had been nodding his head in mechanical agreement, but now he had nothing to say.

So Jackson went on. "Look," he said, "it makes me feel

bad too. I'm not cut out for this business. I should go back to farming. I was a pretty good farmer."

Fogarty breathed in the air conditioning that floated up out of the slot in the window. "Why'd you quit?" he asked.

"Hay fever," said Jackson. "She's the one who calls herself Sparkle, right?"

"Yes," said Fogarty.

"Cute? About nineteen?"

"Eighteen," said Fogarty.

"What else do we know about her? If I remember correctly, that's the same name she used on the rental agreement."

Jackson remembered right; Fogarty had already checked. The rental agreement had been signed in the winter, just before Fogarty had become apartment manager.

"At least we should try to get hold of her real name," said Jackson. "What if she tries to skip out on us?"

Fogarty considered this as he watched the two girls argue about who should get the earphones now. It was sad. They were both pulling at the earphones, pulling them apart. Soon they would break. "Jesus, it's hot," he said suddenly, backing away from the car, blinking at the sun. "Look, what I'll do is keep an eye out. I see everything that happens around here."

"Right. And see if you can get her real name. For two months' rent it would be worth tracking her down."

"Yeah," said Fogarty, "sure," trying to imagine the dogs, noses to the ground, hot on the track, the trail – hot after the sweet flowery scent – of Sparkle.

o

He went to find Vargo. Vargo carried the mail by day and painted pictures by night. Oil on canvas.

Each afternoon Vargo could be found, after his route, at the Hi-Brau, holding court, drinking cheap whiskey, and bitching, mostly about the government.

"Shit," Fogarty could hear Vargo saying as he stepped in out of the sun, "the next thing you know they'll have us in a safe little war. You watch. There are too many generals out of work."

"The dog kicking the master again?" said Fogarty, having come up quietly behind Vargo at the bar. "You're in uniform yourself, you know."

It was true. Vargo had changed his shirt, but he was still wearing his regulation gray summer shorts with the black stripes. Now he pivoted on the stool and appeared before Fogarty with his palm raised, as though he had been expecting precisely that comment from an unseen quarter.

"I am the loyal opposition," he said. "It is my duty to oppose and protest. You know what I saw yesterday? I'll tell you. Four guys on one city truck, counting potholes. Not fixing them, counting them. Not one, but four. And moving slow."

"Unlike yourself," said Fogarty, glad for the musty coolness of the Hi-Brau.

"Unlike myself," said Vargo, "who walks more than eight miles every day over cracked sidewalks covered with dogshit and mean morning drunks. Not to mention the famous weather over which we always triumph. Have a drink." He signaled the bartender.

Vargo's complaints were never new, only the details changed.

"So why don't you quit?" said Fogarty. A beer appeared. It was a ritual question. The answers varied.

"Art," Vargo said today. "I have my art to feed. Paint and canvas to buy. I think of my job as a blind government grant. They don't know what I'm doing with their money."

Fogarty thought of Vargo's paintings, colorful but violent abstractions, natural extensions of his political thought. Vargo was ultimately an anarchist. It was already time to change the subject.

"Hot today," said Fogarty.

"Hotter than a five-dollar ten-speed," said Vargo. "Which reminds me. You need a color television? One of the people on my route has a warm Sony he'd let go for a song."

"Sorry, the only song I'm singing is the billfold blues." Which reminded Fogarty of the main reason he had sought out Vargo today. "But where is it?" he asked. "Just in case."

"Guy on Eighth Avenue right down the street from you."

"That's terrific, burglars just around the corner." Fogarty took a thoughtful drink of his beer. "You meet them all, don't you? Crooks, crazies, naked ladies."

"Not enough of the last." Something resembling a smile began to spread on Vargo's face. "You're leading up to something."

"Maybe. You deliver to the Newgate, don't you?"

"That falling-down piece of shit called a building which you allegedly manage? Yes."

"You know apartment number five, at the end of the hall?"

"Young chick with a nice ass and biker friends."

"A biker brother," said Fogarty. He had never before mentioned Sparkle to Vargo. Vargo would tell him that no matter what he was doing with her, he was making a big mistake. "What's her name?" asked Fogarty.

"She's your tenant," said Vargo. "You tell me."

"But she's on your route, right?"

"Okay, I'll bite one time. She goes by Sparkle."

"Yes, but what's her real name?"

"Can't tell you."

"You mean won't?" said Fogarty.

"I mean can't," said Vargo.

"She never gets mail under any other name?"

"Rarely gets mail at all. But naturally I noticed the blue Magic Marker on her box. Cute. Leaves her door open. There's a reason you're asking."

Fogarty looked into his beer, watched the little golden bubbles there, rising. "I may have a problem," he said slowly.

"Hoo boy," said Vargo through his teeth. "Whatever it is, I'll tell you one thing."

"What?"

"You're making a big mistake."

o

That evening Fogarty went across the street to have a talk with Sparkle. He found her on her way out of the building, dressed as usual in her white shorts. Tonight the halter top was a soft blue, punctuated by her small nipples, and she had added a pair of red high-heeled shoes that Fogarty had never seen before. Standing with her hands on her hips in the doorway, she looked like a painted billboard ad for a rock 'n' roll radio station. She'd made up her face to heighten her cheekbones, deepen her eyes, and thicken her lashes, and her long hair showed the sheen of having just been washed. A small leather purse hung by a leather string from her shoulder.

"You're off," he said.

"Me and my feet," she said.

Fogarty grimaced. "Jackson stopped by," he said.

"Yeah?" She was bubbling with good cheer. "Is he going to fix my toilet?"

"He's going to fix *us*," said Fogarty, testing the waters. He needed her to slow down, show him some attention; after all, she was the one in trouble. He was trying to help. He *wanted* to help. She could at least show a little appreciation.

Instead she was oblivious. "Yeah?" she said. "What could he do to us?"

It occurred to Fogarty that she was too young to understand. This did not console him; it angered him. He changed the subject.

"Where are you going?" he asked.

"You said I needed to get hold of some money."

"Spark," he said sternly, "that's not an answer."

"To see what I can do." Now *she* seemed angry. "What business is it of yours?"

"It's my business, for chrissake. It's my business. I'm supposed to give you an eviction notice. I'm supposed to nail it to your fucking door. Today. Tonight. You have until Friday."

She looked at him blankly. "It'll be okay," she said.

What did she mean by that? "Maybe you think you'll be okay," he said, "but what about me? This is my job we're talking about, and I'm not going to have it anymore when you don't pay."

"Jeez, would he really do that?"

"He really would," said Fogarty, sickened with the simple truth of it. Being apartment manager of the Newgate wasn't much, but it was something; and it was all he had. "I'm not just replaceable," he said, "I'm easily replaceable."

Then, to Fogarty's surprise, Sparkle was suddenly down out of the shadowed frame of the door and moving toward him where he stood, braced, on the bottom concrete step; moving sympathetically and sexually; moving like a woman, not a girl.

Fogarty backed off, held her but not tightly. Then he carefully pulled down her hands from his neck to the space he was creating between their bodies. Sparkle turned down her mouth. Fogarty hoped, secretly, that he had hurt her.

"Where are you going?" he said. "Tell me."

"I told you I was working on it." She put on her pout. "I should get some tonight."

"Money?"

"Money."

Fogarty thought about it, the likelihood of it. Of course, all things were possible. "How?" he said.

"Can't tell you."

Won't, he thought. But he didn't push; he wouldn't push; he wasn't going to push. "When?" he said.

"Tonight, I just told you."

"When will you be back?"

"Why?" she said, hands defiantly on her hips again.

"If you bring some money by midnight, maybe I wouldn't have to give you the eviction notice."

"Then I'll be back," she said, more softly. "By midnight."

Fogarty thought about it. "All right." He was encouraged. "I'll be home."

"Your place?"

"We can celebrate," said Fogarty. "I have a bottle of wine."

"Okay, I'll be back," said Sparkle. "Wait up for me."

"Don't worry."

She put her mouth to his, darted her tongue around the rim of his lips. He leaned toward her this time, interested; but she was already moving around him, past him, down the last step and onto the sidewalk. Then she was gone, prancing awkwardly, almost as though tipsy, up the street in her red high-heeled shoes.

o

It only took him until a quarter past twelve to realize she was not going to appear that night at all. What exactly, he wondered, had ever allowed him to think she would?

By one o'clock he had at least established a tentative answer to that question: he had been tricked, he decided, by the fact that she had so obviously not been lying when she said she would be back. He had thus foolishly accepted her innocent projection as the truth. It wasn't the first time he had made that mistake. His was the human error of blind hope compounded by a twitch in his thigh. He admitted it. And hers was the human error of simply not knowing what she was doing. She was young, too young.

Or he was too old. The truth of this did not comfort him; he was not her father.

But like a father he began to worry about her. Every female was, after all, some man's daughter; and it was all too likely that she was out right now trying to trade on her sex. She was quick on her feet despite those high-heeled shoes: more than pretty as a girl, mindful of how to make herself look available as a woman, distressingly accomplished as a lover. And he knew there were plenty of men, both older and younger than he, who would pay well for such a thing. He thought of Jackson; but then it was true that Jackson would first try to get it on credit.

Yes, she was capable of such a thing — with painful reluctance Fogarty had to admit it. Her brother (if blood meant anything) was, after all, a car thief.

But where would she go? She surely didn't have either

the sophistication or the connections necessary to work the lobbies of the downtown hotels, like the Marriott and the Regency; and he couldn't see her walking the streets and bars, she was too bright for that. What was left?

At one-thirty he began to write out the eviction notice. What choice did he have? He followed the form and wording on the state-provided model he found in the folder left behind by the previous apartment manager, a man he had never met. What, wondered Fogarty, had that man's relationship with Sparkle been like? The phantom signature on the rental agreements and old receipts revealed nothing.

Around two, he made his way across the moonlit street, the asphalt still warm beneath his bare feet, the eviction notice rolled up in his hand, his fist.

Inside the darkened building he stopped to listen but heard nothing. He felt like a criminal. Or a cartoon detective. At the end of the hall he stood in front of the imitation brass number five and half expected her to suddenly come up behind him. Surprise him and say, *Hey, I'm back, let's go to your place.*

He could not bring himself to fix the notice to her door. The thumbtack he had brought for that purpose pricked at his finger and finally, feeling foolish, he backed down the hall – or rather turned and crept – to the mailboxes. Even without the hall lights he could easily make out hers. Blue Magic Marker, a child's beautiful scrawl, *Sparkle.*

He slid the notice through the slot. What else could he do? Then he recrossed the street, feeling older than his thirty-nine years, to linger on the gray tattered edge of a half night's sleep.

o

The next morning Fogarty stuck close to home, kept an eye on the Newgate, did not cross the street. He saw no sign of Sparkle. He felt strangely relieved. She had been irresponsible. He had done only what he had to do; it was out of his hands.

Jackson called around noon. Fogarty knew it was Jackson before Jackson actually spoke because of the brief electronic bleep.

"Did you collect the sixty short, from number nine?"

Fogarty had forgotten all about number nine. "Probably later today," he said.

"God I hope so. It's my oldest girl's birthday tomorrow and I should at least get her a stuffed animal or something. Or is that too young for twelve? Tell me the truth, what do you think?"

"It's not something I've thought about," said Fogarty, mentally counting the years between twelve and eighteen. The small number disturbed him.

"God," said Jackson, "I shouldn't have had so many kids. And all of them girls. Girls cost more. I can't even afford my wife. Did you put the notice up on five?"

"Yes," said Fogarty, "she has until Friday."

o

Exhausted from having done so little all day, and still without a sign of Sparkle, Fogarty walked in the late afternoon heat of the city to the Hi-Brau. Vargo was there, basking in the cool dark, holding the palm of his hand in the air.

"If there was no government," he was saying, "then there would be no taxes. And without government there would be no war. We would have no organized destructive capability, so as a people we would represent no threat. It's as simple as that. And we wouldn't have to take a cut in our standard of living because an absence of government does not cancel out capitalism."

"Who would build the roads?" asked Fogarty from the door. "Who would deliver the mail?"

"Roads have always been built. Important messages have always been delivered." Vargo spun around on his barstool. "It would be a free market. Where there's a need, there will always be someone prepared to meet it. For a price."

"Who would protect you from thieves, cutthroats, murderers?"

"Who protects me now?"

A beer arrived at the bar for Fogarty. He decided to let Vargo's politics drift on the air. "It's another hot one out there today," he said.

"Hotter than buck night at the cathouse," said Vargo.

Fogarty began to wish he had stayed home; Vargo's chatter did not distract him, it only tightened him up.

"Know what I saw today? I'll tell you. I saw a city government pickup hauling a speedboat. Right down Sixth Avenue. About noon. Two guys in the front, two in the back. One in the boat. I ask you, is this where my tax dollar should go?"

Fogarty opened his mouth and let it close. He had nothing to say.

"You're too quiet," said Vargo. "That's the way people get when they've made a mistake. There's no sparkle in your eye."

Fogarty could see it coming.

Vargo leaned forward, narrowed his vision, and poked his finger into Fogarty's chest. "I saw your eviction notice," he said, "in her mailbox."

"What," said Fogarty, "were you doing in her mailbox?"

"My job. I was delivering the mail."

"She got a letter?" There was hope.

"You bet she got a letter," said Vargo. "She got a letter that suggested its contents might well mean a large sum of money." Vargo paused, poked again, though not as hard. "And it was not, I might add, simply addressed to a Sparkle."

Fogarty breathed deeply. He did not trust Vargo. You couldn't trust an anarchist. "But you're not going to tell me who it was to or who it was from, is that correct?"

"To do so would be to betray the trust the public has placed in me," said Vargo. "I'll tell you for a drink."

Fogarty sighed, got the bartender's attention, pointed at Vargo's empty glass, and settled back.

Vargo waited for his whiskey to arrive, stirred down the ice with his finger, then licked the finger. Finally he took a deliberate sip.

"The letter," he said, "was from the Irish Sweepstakes." He put on his most official face. "It was addressed to Occupant."

o

Sparkle appeared, at Fogarty's door and to Fogarty's surprise, just before midnight that night. She was carrying her red high-heeled shoes in her hand by their thin straps, and tears brimmed from her eyes, which had been cleansed of mascara. Fogarty let her in, sat her down, but was resolved to keep his distance.

"I got the money," she said, "but now it's gone. Can I stay with you tonight?"

"You're exactly twenty-four hours late," he said.

"I know that," she said. "I know. I haven't even been home yet."

Then she hasn't seen the notice, thought Fogarty. Tears ran freely down her face. "What happened?" he asked.

"I borrowed the money from a friend of mine, who sells furniture, you know, used. Well, hot. Four hundred. But I had to wait until this morning to get it, and then when I did I decided to go see my parents because it breaks me up that we don't get along. I took them some groceries with some of the money."

Fogarty sat down next to her on the couch. Then he stood up again. Out of the corner of his eye — through the window and across the street in front of the Newgate — he saw an old and battered pickup truck come to a slow rolling stop. He had never seen it before. Somehow it was suspicious.

He saw all this as he turned to switch off the lamp at the end of the couch that glared in Sparkle's sad, wet face. In the relative darkness he sat back down beside her. "Go on," he said.

"Only my dad was home. He can't work anymore because

31

of his back, you know. My mother was out cleaning some-body's house. My dad said he was glad to see me, but that it was a bad day because the police had called about my brother. They were ready to release him on bond, but nobody had enough money."

Fogarty could see it coming. "So you contributed yours," he said.

She nodded affirmatively, wiped at her tears. It was impos-sible not to believe her. Only the pickup bothered him. Fogarty felt himself yielding, yet could not bring himself to comfort her fully. "That was a dumb thing to do," he heard himself say.

"No it wasn't," she wailed at him. "He's my brother, my big brother; it felt good to be able to help him. You should understand that."

Fogarty tried to make the best of his insensitivity. After a minute he said, "At least you'll get your money back."

"No I won't."

"Why not? They only hold the bond, they don't keep it."

"They keep it if you leave it."

"He's running out on the bond?"

"He left at noon. He should be five hundred miles from here by now."

"That's terrible," said Fogarty. "That's rotten."

"No it's not." Sparkle stared at him damply. He was obvi-ously being stupid. "How would you like to go to prison?" she said.

Fogarty gave in. What was the point of resistance? "Okay, Spark," he said, "if it's not so bad that you gave away your rent money so your brother could skip out on the law and on you, then why are you crying?"

She looked at him incredulously. "You see these?" she said, holding up the red high-heeled shoes before his face. "I broke them. Both of them. Coming up *your* front steps. See?"

What Fogarty saw was that they were very cheaply made and that the spike heel on one and the strap on the other were indeed broken. How had she managed it? And meanwhile, in the course of showing him the shoes, she had somehow snuggled her small frame into his on the couch – made herself tiny, defenseless – and he was caressing her hair, feeling her heat, was all too aware of the smell of her. How had she managed it?

"Can I stay with you?" she said softly. "Just for tonight?"

Fogarty did not have to think about it. "No," he said, and meant it. But even as he spoke he could not stop stroking her hair; and it was hard, a few minutes later, to watch from his darkened window as she slowly crossed the empty, brightly lit street.

He watched sadly, with real concern; and for a moment it seemed clear to him that she too was apprehensive about the pickup truck, in which a cigarette glowed behind the steering wheel. But then suddenly her walk accelerated and she was herself by the truck, at the driver's window, leaning forward, blocking the pinpoint of red; and when she moved away from the truck a moment later, it was with a nod at the driver.

She went into the Newgate. Fogarty watched as more light, this time from Sparkle's kitchen window at the back of the building, suddenly illuminated a square patch of green grass. And watched as the figure behind the wheel of the truck got out, dropped his cigarette to the ground, and also went inside. Fogarty could not see him well, but well enough to make out that it was a man of middle age; a man at least as old as Fogarty; a man old enough to be Sparkle's father.

o

All the next day the truck did not move from its spot at the curb. Nor did Fogarty move from his place on his couch, where he rested in fitful vigilance until nearly noon when Jackson bleeped.

"It's Thursday," said Jackson, "my oldest daughter's birthday. What have we got from nine?"

Once again Fogarty had forgotten about nine. He should

have gone over there last night, made some demands.

"I went over there last night," he said, "and made some demands. They said later today or tomorrow. I'll call you."

"No. I'd better come by. I'm desperate. Even a twenty would help. What's a birthday party without cake and ice cream? She's got a crowd coming. My wife will kill me. I should have stayed on the farm. And Sparkle in five. Did she get the notice?"

"I don't think she's been home."

"Haven't you been over there? Maybe you should go over there."

"I twisted my ankle," said Fogarty, thinking of high-heeled shoes. "I haven't moved all morning."

"I'd better come by," said Jackson.

Fogarty could see that it was hot outside. Much too hot. He didn't want to have anything to do with this, with any part of it. But an hour later, just as he heard the phone ring and saw the white Jaguar pull up behind the battered pickup, he also saw Vargo, loping down the street from the opposite direction, a half-full bag of mail at his shoulder. And Fogarty, feigning a limp, went out into the heat to meet them both.

Jackson was just climbing out of his car when Fogarty arrived beside him.

"You didn't answer," said the landlord.

"That's because I'm here," said Fogarty.

There were no kids in the back this time, but Fogarty did notice Vargo ducking with a grin into the Newgate.

"Well," said Jackson, "no time like the present."

Fogarty hobbled behind him at a short distance. It's out of my hands, he was thinking. I haven't done a thing, there was nothing I could do.

They met Vargo at the mailboxes, just relocking the box designated by blue Magic Marker.

"She got a letter?" said Fogarty.

"You're an observant person," said the mailman.

"Who was it addressed to?" asked Jackson.

Vargo turned slowly on the building's owner. "Do you

realize," he said, "that giving you that information is a federal offense? Do you want me to go to prison? And don't offer me money," he added, holding up his hand, "because that would make you guilty of trying to bribe a government official." Then he was gone, out the door and lumbering down the street in his heavy hiking boots.

"He's just the sort of thing that's wrong with this country," said Jackson dejectedly as he walked the hall to number five. Fogarty watched from the mailboxes.

Jackson knocked on Sparkle's door. There was no answer. Then he pounded on it. Still there was no answer.

"I'll probably have to turn my kids over to a state agency before this is over," he said, starting up the stairs. "Or maybe I could advertise for foster homes. They're not ugly, not badly behaved. Just a little underfed."

Fogarty could hear him knock, then pound, at number nine above. Nothing. Back at the bottom of the stairs, a moment later, he again tried five; but the entire building was silent.

"Damn, and I drove clear over here. Now what am I going to do?" What he did shocked Fogarty; Jackson actually took the silk handkerchief out of his breast pocket and mopped his sweaty brow with it. "I'm tempted to skip town," he said, "but I can't afford the gas."

Back outside, beneath the sun, they stood at the Jaguar.

"At least we can presume she got the notice," said Jackson, "since it's not on her door."

"Presumably," said Fogarty.

"What's this truck?" said Jackson.

"I don't know," said Fogarty. "Never seen it before."

"What a piece of junk. It makes the whole neighborhood look bad. No wonder I can't keep anything rented around here."

"Something should happen soon," said Fogarty, without the slightest idea of what it might be.

"Well, keep on it," said Jackson, climbing back into the car. "Keep an eye out. Watch for funny stuff. And give me a call. You know I'm desperate."

"I know you're desperate," said Fogarty, but the Jaguar had already pulled around the truck and was gone.

o

Had they been in there all the time? How had she known not to answer the door when Jackson knocked? Were they in there now? Or had they left earlier in the morning, on foot, and he, Fogarty, missed them? And, in any case, who was that man?

Fogarty sat on his own front stoop watching the street go by. Above him the sun inched through a hazy cloudless sky. Across the street, the pickup did not move at all.

Fogarty did not leave the front stoop all afternoon except to refill his glass with iced tea; did not, as he had earlier thought he might, wander down to the Hi-Brau. Vargo would only have more fun at his expense. But that wasn't it; Fogarty did not leave the stoop because he couldn't, was compelled by some inner strength or weakness to stand guard over these final proceedings, the end of whatever was happening, an end that he knew was near.

He saw the people in nine arrive home – man, woman, and unhappy child – but did not bother with them; and when the phone rang around six he did not answer it. No doubt it was Jackson, anxious to tell him to keep an eye out, to go try Sparkle's door. But Jackson's deadline was tomorrow night. Friday. This was only Thursday. He counted the rings. Eight, then a long pause and eight more. Jackson for sure.

An hour later Vargo came by. "I tried to call," he said, "about an hour ago. You didn't answer."

"Taking a shower," said Fogarty.

"I thought you ought to know about it," said Vargo.

"Know about what?"

"The letter I put in her box."

Fogarty felt tired, bone-tired. "What about it?"

"It could just be the answer to your question."

36

"The question of her name?"

"Indeed," said Vargo.

"What's the charge?"

"Charge? You're a friend. In trouble. In need. Don't insult me."

"Then just tell me."

"How about a drink first?"

"All I've got is iced tea."

"Want to smoke a little dope?"

"I just want to sit here."

"Okay," said Vargo, "it's your funeral. Two names — first and last."

"Which you're not going to tell me, right?"

"I'm telling you," said Vargo. "It's Star."

"Star?" It wasn't possible. Fogarty had once, a long time ago, known a woman named Brett Starr. "What was the first name?" he asked.

"That is the first name," said Vargo.

Fogarty halfheartedly turned it around. "Star? Star what?"

"Bright," said Vargo. "Star Bright."

"Fuck you," said Fogarty.

"Please. I checked the phone book. There are twenty-four Brights listed in this town. Why not a Star? Why not?"

"Look," said Fogarty. "I don't care if her name is Aurora Borealis. Okay?"

"Then why are you sitting here?"

"I don't know."

"Here," said Vargo, "you'd better take this." He handed Fogarty a fat yellow joint. "I think you're going to need it." And left.

o

The sky finally began to fade. Fogarty sat and waited, nursed his iced tea, sat, waited. He did not smoke the joint. Street traffic slowed, but nothing changed across the street. When it was finally dark he went inside, but only to take up his post at the window.

Where he sat and waited, waited and sat; until, after an hour, he saw the first sign. The light in Sparkle's kitchen, at the back of the building, went on. Then, after another half hour, another sign: an old Chevrolet van, large and square and as battered as the pickup, pulled up in front of the Newgate. A man of maybe thirty and a girl with feathers in her hair went into the building. Fogarty had never seen either of them before, but he knew where they were going.

When the phone rang, he accidentally answered it. It was Jackson.

"Have you been over there, tried her door?"

"There's no one home."

"How do you know?"

"There aren't any lights on."

"She'd better come home. She only has until tomorrow midnight."

"I'm sure she knows."

When the connection went bad, Fogarty let it stay bad. That happened with car phones. An indistinct Jackson, behind a panel of static, finally hung up. Tried to call back. Fogarty ignored the ringing, wondered how the birthday party had been.

From his window he saw another sign. Two loud motorcycles pulled up behind the van. Each had two riders, a male at the handlebars and a female clinging to the male. All sexes wore leather. The evening, thought Fogarty, was much too warm for leather. Again Fogarty recognized no one, and again they all disappeared into the Newgate.

That made eight of them, Fogarty calculated. What were they doing in there? Perhaps he should go over, now, before it was too late. Give himself up. It would not be so hard, he thought, to deliver himself into Sparkle's hands. He could join them. After tomorrow he would be out of a job, free to start a new life.

But he did not—could not—move from his place at the window.

No one left, no one came out. Nearly an hour passed.

Now it was almost eleven. Fogarty was exhausted, yet so dry-eyed that he could not blink. He felt like an overcharged battery. His vision was fixed. His scalp itched.

Then it happened. An old station wagon of indistinct make came to a screeching halt behind the line of motorcycles, behind the van, behind the pickup truck. The door of the station wagon flew open; a small middle-aged woman leaped out into the street and slammed the door. Here was authority. The woman wore coveralls and her hair was tucked up into a blue knit stocking cap. She was built like a refrigerator. She did not walk or run toward the building, she assaulted it.

This was it. Fogarty refilled his glass with iced tea, went back outside to sit on the front stoop. He would be there as long as he had to be. He felt he was going to the opening of a movie in which he had played a starring role; he had earned his front-row seat.

He did not have to wait long. A few minutes later one of the leather-clad men emerged from the building and hurried on foot down the street. In less than ten minutes he was back with a case of beer, which he transferred from his shoulder to the top of the station wagon. Then he went back into the Newgate, but only for a moment, and when he reappeared he was not alone. He and one of the other men were carrying Sparkle's couch. The girl with the feathers followed behind them with a lamp. The couch was placed in the far back of the pickup, facing the raised tailgate.

Others had taken off their leather jackets. This was hot, hard work. Tables and chairs, a mattress and box springs and stereo speakers, plants and a potted tree, pictures and posters and overflowing cardboard boxes all appeared in a frightening outpour.

Fogarty counted eight people, all working hard, except for the older man in a dirty scoop-necked T-shirt and stubbled beard, whom Fogarty recognized as the driver of the pickup. He was doing nothing at all. Only Sparkle herself was missing.

The older woman stood by her station wagon, dispensing

beer as people completed their third and fourth loads. The side doors of the van had been opened, as well as the back of the station wagon. Some items were immediately loaded – onto or into one of the vehicles, according to the woman's directions – while others were deposited on the grass between the curb and the sidewalk.

Fogarty wondered, of course, if they recognized him for who he was. Certainly they could see him, as easily as he could see them. Either way, they gave him no notice.

The loading up was not frantic, but under the older woman's hand it was deliberate, orderly, efficient. And fast. A second round of beer was handed out before the final boxes, bags, and sheeted bundles were transferred from the grass to the vehicles. The pickup truck was full, overflowing. Everything was stacked high, packed between the cab and the couch in the back, but the rigging of ropes made everything appear secure.

And Fogarty thought, I should call Jackson, I should call the police, knowing that he would do neither. I should go over there, at least – tell them I see what they are doing and it is wrong. But he was not so sure it was.

They had, after all, come to get her.

He watched. Until everything was loaded, last beer dispensed with loud healthy pops in the still night air; until everyone had moved to some final station. Watched until the kitchen light in the back went out and, a moment later, Sparkle appeared at the front of the building, framed in the light at the Newgate's front door.

For an instant she did not move, seemed to be surveying her transported world and dutiful subjects at a careful distance. Then the hall light too went out.

She was dressed as always in white shorts and halter top. The high-heeled shoes had either been thrown away or packed in one of the boxes. She moved on bare feet across the grass. There was no question but that she saw Fogarty – her eyes did not leave him as she floated across the lawn – and for a moment he believed she was coming to him.

For him? He wished it.

But her destination was only the pickup truck, the couch at the back, to which she was hoisted by one of the men. Sitting on it, one leg slung over the other, she seemed theatrically at ease — as everyone else began, one by one, to disappear into their vehicles or mount their bikes. The caravan was nearly ready to roll.

Six doors slammed shut. And then, as though the waiting city itself expected a final sign, all was quiet one last time.

Sparkle sat on the couch, looking at Fogarty, who was looking back. The sixty feet between them was nothing. Fogarty could feel her eyes, their heat, could nearly count the beat of her regular heart. And then, clearly enough, he heard her voice.

"We fixed the toilet," she said through the still night air. "It was no big deal. The keys are in the mailbox." There was no triumph in her voice, no noticeable satisfaction; but if there was sorrow, that too was hidden.

Then the older woman's arm appeared out of the station wagon's window and waved itself emphatically in the air. This was the signal of a confident woman, a certain mother.

All engines were started; and then the procession, beneath a fat red moon that had just appeared over the Newgate's roof, was slowly moving off into the hot city night. Sparkle was going home.

Soon Fogarty could no longer see the procession's taillights — although for a time he could still hear the sound of the motorcycle engines, sucking up more and more of the scarce city air. Then even the sound was gone and Fogarty knew that he should go in.

But he could not move yet. Inside he would be alone — outside the swollen moon would feel familiar, comforting.

Santorini Gray

Here we found ourselves naked, holding
the scales that tipped toward
injustice.

> — George Seferis,
> from "Santorini"

THEY STOOD ON rain-soaked gravel, his arm loosely around her waist, watching the Greek driver tinker with the engine of the hulking black taxi.

"Nice night for the trip," said David, ending a long silence. "You'll be able to make out the islands all the way to Athens if you stay awake."

The late summer storm, which for two days had kept boats from the island, had passed. The full moon cast thick black shadows and turned lingering puddles to obsidian.

"It'll be cold," she said. "It'll be cold and damp and I won't be able to sleep, period."

David could see her. Alone and cold and bitter, huddled in her navy blue pea coat on one of the forward decks of the *Oia*. If there were many passengers, she wouldn't even have a bench to herself but would have to sit up for the entire twelve hours. Christ, he thought, why did I have to get her deck passage? It was unkind enough that he wasn't going

43

with her to Athens, to see her off at the airport.

"Look, maybe we can still get you a berth. Sometimes they save them back. Or maybe there's been a cancellation. When we get down to the pier we'll check, okay?"

"I'll live," she said, tightening her lips.

Suffer, you mean. You'll suffer mightily and need to remind me now because I won't be there later.

He watched as the last piece of luggage was hoisted to the top of the taxi and the driver began securing the load with a length of blond rope; dark hands weaving the line through leather and plastic and cardboard grips until they came to the long canvas straps of Darcy's two bags.

Big, shapeless canvas bags that zippered shut. The brown one on which she had painted a smiling dragon, because dragons are good luck, David. Stuffed with two changes of clothing and the pea coat with its anchor buttons. The other one, the faded yellow one, filled with long-stemmed brushes and charcoal pencils, her collection of cheap silver rings and bracelets and earrings, the big Dali book, sketches and unfilled canvases rolled inside cardboard tubes. Crazy canvas bags that he told her she was crazy to buy, because they had no body, wouldn't hold up. What do you mean, no body? she had asked. Don't be stupid, he had said.

In an hour the bags would be gone, she would be gone, it would be over.

"You should say goodbye to Lefteris," he said. The double doors of the taxi were open and David could see people already sitting inside. "They'll wait for us."

He led Darcy around to the back of the café, choosing not the muddy path but a route over a thick mat of silver leaves beneath storm-beaten olive trees. In the smoky kitchen the old Greek's bare torso was nearly lost in an open oven. They watched from the door as he removed two steaming trays of *pastitsio* and dropped them to a counter. When he turned to face them he was already smiling his best sad smile.

"You are leaving?" His gray stubbled cheeks glistened with sweat.

They nodded.

"Perhaps the weather keeps the *Oia* in Crete still." His words were just for Darcy now. "Perhaps you must return to me tonight."

"I hope not," David said too quickly. Then: "The sky is clear."

Lefteris wiped his dark fingers on his soiled apron, studied Darcy's face.

"You won't forget my Santorini?" he said, stepping forward, placing his thick hands on either side of Darcy's small face; lifting it, framing it. Darcy's eyes flashed from Lefteris to David, back to Lefteris. Her goodbye smile became smaller, rounder. She said nothing. "You won't forget?" The old man's breath, David knew, would be rich with garlic and the licorice smell of ouzo.

"I won't forget," said Darcy.

Outside the taxi's horn sounded.

"We'd better go," said David.

Bending forward, Lefteris kissed the girl on the cheek and the forehead, then abruptly turned back to his smoking oven.

The huge taxi was nearly full. Next to the driver in the front sat a heavy middle-aged couple, a young boy wedged between them. Their patient silence said they were Greek. In the back sat six well-dressed young men, laughing and talking loudly in German. David and Darcy took the only remaining places, facing each other next to the door. Over the small, enforced distance he could feel the heat of her eyes. The driver lit a cigarette.

Stop it. Don't stare at me like that. I didn't plan this, it wasn't my fault. Things die and it's nobody's fault.

He looked away, out the taxi. Above the café a wavering point of light grew to fill a square, the window of the little room where they had so many times watched in reverse this scene of a departing taxi. The cloth wick, floating in a shallow pan of oil, always burned in their absence. To give us a sense of place, he had told her. Now it seemed all wrong, inappropriately bright.

"Okay?" asked the driver, pivoting his woolly head to survey his eleven passengers.

"Okay," echoed the Germans, slamming the double doors on their side, passing a bottle among themselves as they continued to snicker at some private amusement.

Drunk. Just like a bunch of Krauts to be drunk all the way home from their drunken holiday.

The driver started the engine and the heavy machine lumbered away from the café. The Germans cheered. For a kilometer or more the gravel road pursued the gray pebble beach, bearing the litter of the storm: torn seaweed and dead fish that could be better smelled than seen. On the other side of the road weathered blue and white stucco boathouses appeared and disappeared under the low moon.

"What if Lefteris was right?" said Darcy. "What if the boat isn't coming tonight?"

"The driver would know that."

"Sure, but why should he tell us? By keeping quiet he doesn't lose the fare for taking us to Phira and doubles it by bringing us back. Very neat."

"You don't trust anyone."

"I trusted you," she said. The stare again.

If the *Oia* didn't come tonight it would probably drop back to its regular weekly schedule and wouldn't come again for another four days. The prospect settled like acid on David's stomach. They had been together on the island for a year. Before that he had lived alone in the little room above Lefteris's. Convinced of his loneliness, he had written her. It is Atlantis, he told her. I need to share it. I need you. In her fourth ærogram she agreed to join him before the end of summer. Sometime in the rainy winter he had stopped needing her. If the *Oia* didn't come tonight, it would be another four days before she could leave.

David felt a poke to his shoulder and looking up met the eyes of the German next to Darcy, who was grinning and yelling across the narrow aisle as though volume might compensate for their language difference. The sounds bounced uselessly off David's thoughts and he leaned back, hoping to escape. But the German followed David's retreat. Crouched on his haunches between the seats. Steadied himself against David's knee. "Change," he said now in English, pointing at the cushion he had just left. "Change."

"It's okay," said David, understanding at last. "It's okay just like this."

"Okay, okay," grinned the German, making insistent lifting motions with his free hand. "Change."

David felt a fine spray of spittle hit his face. He would do as the German wanted; he would have done more to keep things pleasant. It was easiest that way. Quickly he shifted to the place beside Darcy.

"Asshole," he said to the German, covering his pronouncement with a smile.

"Lovers," said the German to David and Darcy, then "*Sie sind Liebhaber*" to the other Germans who smiled and pointed, delighted with the show.

"You didn't want to sit next to me, did you?"

"Darcy, what do you suppose it is that makes them act like that?"

"It's true. You can't stand to be near me. Admit it."

"Would you say it's because they feel they have to live up to their rotten reputation? Would you say that?"

The driver hadn't turned on the headlights. There was no need for them. White gravel crunched evenly beneath the wheels.

"Lovers, that's a laugh. The last time we made love you might as well have been at a funeral."

He reached for her face, he wasn't sure why. She moved, but not soon enough.

"Your cheek is hot. Are you too warm? It's warm in here. I'll roll down a window."

"No."

"Are you cold?"

"No."

The taxi slowed, turned off the gravel and away from the

sea. From here it was twelve kilometers of barely perceptible ascent to Phira, the tiny port city perched above the harbor on the other side of the island. The road would be in bad shape, David knew that. When it was dry it was little more than a winding dirt path; when it rained it became a gummy river of mud.

"It's going to be a mess," he said. "A real shitty mess."

"I'm sorry."

"It's not your fault."

"I mean I'm sorry I said those things."

"With this load on we're bound to have trouble."

Low stone walls lined the road. Beyond them stretched tomato fields. If the road was a river of mud, the fields were seas of the same, and the stone walls, like dikes, kept one from the other.

"It's just that I still don't understand why I'm leaving."

"Look at that mud, Darcy. Just look at it." The driver had turned on the headlights.

"Listen to me."

"It's going to be a bitch. A real bitch."

David felt another jab to his shoulder. This time it was the German next to him, thrusting a bottle at his face. "*Trink*," he was saying, rolling back his head and jerking his thumb at his own open mouth. David pushed the bottle away.

"*Trink.*"

"Asshole."

"*Ja, der Schnaps, guter Schnaps*," and again the bottle was extended. The other Germans watched, smiled, nodded.

David could feel little saline beads rising on his forehead, his chest, the back of his neck. For a moment he could see it clearly. They were all in on this, out to bust his head apart like a vase thrown at a wall.

"*Trink*," demanded the German. David seized the bottle and put it to his lips. On the third swallow he choked. The Germans applauded.

"What's wrong?" asked Darcy.

"They tried to poison me."

"Not with you, with the car."

David looked out the window. They weren't moving.

"We're stuck," he said. "We're stuck in the goddamn mud."

The big tires began churning the road: forward, reverse, forward, reverse. The taxi slid sideways, toward the stone fence. David glanced at Darcy. Small hands covered her face.

Something caught beneath the wheels, or one of the wheels, and they were backing down the road. After a hundred yards they stopped.

"Okay?" asked the driver without turning his head.

"Okay," chorused the six Germans.

The taxi moved forward, slowly at first, then picked up speed. David squinted at the bad stretch ahead, a dip in the road that wouldn't dry for days. The driver obviously planned to make it through purely on momentum.

This time the taxi hit the sludge like an icebreaker. Throwing a dirty spray behind, it plowed effortlessly through and continued up the road without slowing down. The Germans congratulated one another and passed the bottle of schnaps among themselves.

"Hey Darcy, would you say that was well done? Finely executed? Would you say that?"

"No."

"What's wrong, don't you feel well?"

"No."

"Too hot? I'll roll down that window now."

"No."

"Your stomach. Is it your stomach?"

"We'll get stuck again, won't we?"

He considered it. There was no time to get stuck again. There was no time for anything.

"What's going to happen?" She leaned close.

"How do I know? Am I a prophet?" As he spoke, the back of the taxi began to sway from side to side.

"To us, David. What's going to happen to us?"

Us? There would be no more us. Didn't she understand that yet? That it was over?

"We'll write," he said.

"Write?"

"Make plans."

"What kind of plans?"

He hadn't thought about it. Where he might go, alone. There was Africa, he'd always wanted to go to Africa. Later, when the *Oia* was gone, he would have plenty of time to think about it.

That wouldn't be much longer, they should be close to Phira by now. As he turned his head to look for lights, the taxi suddenly swerved, began to bounce and rock like a plane in a storm. His head hit the roof. There was the sound of breaking glass. A final jolt brought the German across from him down on David's lap.

The taxi no longer moved.

For a moment there was silence, even the engine was still. Then the Germans began to recover loudly and smooth themselves. A couple of them laughed crazily. One was shouting and pointing at the broken schnaps bottle on the floor, another resumed the halting tempo of a drinking song. David could hear moaning, low and steady, coming from the front.

"Okay?" yelled the driver.

There was no unison this time, and the response was slow. But still it came: "Okay."

"Are you all right?" David asked Darcy.

"I guess so. My neck hurts a little. And I think my nose is bleeding."

"Open the door. I want to see what's happened."

"I can't. We're up against the wall."

David turned to the Germans. There was no point in trying to make them understand. He began to climb between their bodies, to get to the other door. "*Liebhaber*," said one of them, thumping him hard on the back. "Lover," a second echoed. "*Trink?*" asked a third, uncapping a new bottle of liquor.

He stepped out into the gray mud. Not far ahead he could see the lights of Phira, gleaming in the freshly washed air.

The road sucked at his sandaled feet as he made his way to the back of the taxi.

The moonlight made it easy for him to study the sink in the road, farther back, where mud had collected rain by rain and year by year until its accumulated mass had broken the ancient stone fence and like lava drained out over the tomato field. Only the rugged roadbed that had been the taxi's undoing was left. David fingered the tender area on his scalp.

The driver appeared to glare at the derailed and tilting taxi and make sad angry noises between his teeth. The night had grown colder. Then, glancing at David, the Greek bent forward and spat twice at the entrenched machine. Don't look at me, David read the message, it wasn't my fault. I was only driving.

The Germans too had left their seats and now stood watching from the middle of the road.

Push, the driver indicated with his hands. "Okay, okay?" Then, affecting confidence, smiling assurances, slogged his way back to his station.

The Germans held a hasty conference in the middle of the road before stepping carefully through the mud to join David. Together they lowered their shoulders to the back of the taxi. The tires spun, they pushed, mud splattered over expensive trousers, they pushed, the taxi sank tighter to the wall. David smelled something burning.

The only movement the taxi made was down. David watched the bumper reach for the road and considered the machine's sinking chances of making it to Phira.

He deserted the Germans. Went around to the side of the taxi. From the running board he climbed to the front fender, where he could easily reach Darcy's two bags. He unbuckled the canvas straps, pushed apart ropes, and pulled first the brown then the faded yellow bag from the chrome frame of the luggage rack.

With one bag under each arm, he dropped back to the road. Inside he could see Darcy huddled against the far door, her hands knotted on her lap and her head bent forward.

"We're going," he called over the whine of the spinning tires. "Come on."

"Going? Going where?" Her voice was distant. She didn't look up.

"Now just where might you suppose, Darcy? To the port maybe? To the boat maybe?" David checked himself, softened his tone. "We'll have to hurry. We don't have much time."

He placed the two bags on the running board and refastened the straps. Darcy began to slide slowly across the plastic-covered seat. David looped the straps over his head so that one bag hung at each hip, a large canvas X appearing across his chest. When she was close enough, he reached for Darcy's hand and pulled her from the taxi. Her nose was still bleeding. There was a dark stain on her peasant blouse. The taxi rocked feebly in the four pits it continued to dig.

"I think we should wait here," said Darcy.

"There's no time for waiting."

"The lady in front, I think she's hurt."

"Are we medics? Come on." They started away from the taxi, David towing at arm's length the girl whose small plodding feet left not holes but channels in the dark mud.

Behind him he could hear shouting, angry Greek shouting, and guessed it was the driver demanding his fare. He would be waving his arms and beating the sky, but David did not turn to see.

He walked fast, trying to keep to the least muddy parts of the road, often choosing the deep ruts the taxi had left earlier, coming down the island. The bags flopped at his sides and their weight pulled at his shoulders. The canvas straps worked the thin material on his T-shirt back and forth, over and into his skin.

For long minutes he focused on the lights ahead. Phira. He could not keep them from moving, coming close to where he thought he might easily put one out with a thrown stone, then receding. Whenever it occurred to him he walked faster. Darcy became another weight, like the bags, another resistance, like the mud. At times he could not have identified the sloshing sound behind him. When she fell he couldn't understand at first what had happened, what had slipped from his hand.

"Goddamn," he said, confused, as though he were the one who had fallen.

She had pitched straight forward, face down into the road. When David crouched to help her up, the bags, too, settled in the mud. Lifting her to her knees he wiped her face with the bottom of his shirt and pushed back her hair. Her eyes opened wide and green and afraid.

"Why are you doing this to me?" she asked.

"Doing to you? I'm not doing anything to you. You fell, that's all. You've got to be more careful. You've got to walk faster."

"I can't."

"You have to. You will." He looked at her hard, pulled her to her feet.

"My sandals, they're full of mud and make me trip."

"So take them off." He should have thought of it before. He would take his own off too. He undid his belt and strung the four dirty sandals around his waist.

Now as they walked the mud rose coldly between their toes. Ahead the lights of Phira became brighter. Single lights grew, divided, multiplied. Angular silhouettes of low buildings appeared and sharpened. A thin trail of ashen smoke, rising from the stack of the tomato cannery, drifted across the white of the moon.

Darcy's small hand was hot and sweaty in his own, and David tried not to hear, behind him, her jagged breathing. Instead he listened for the low electrical hum of the island generator, just ahead, that would mean the end of the tomato fields, the end of the mud, the beginning of Phira. As they walked the drone grew louder, swelling to fill the cool night, yet did not cover his sudden awareness of a new, intruding sound. A honking horn.

David spun around. The big taxi was charging up the

road, coming at them like a war machine. He grabbed Darcy by the waist and pulled her to the wall. With the backs of his legs against the cold stone, he watched as the taxi approached, swerving only slightly from the rutted track when it was nearly upon them. Too late David realized the driver's intent, too late to tell Darcy to close her mouth as he barely managed to cover his own face with his hands. The taxi roared by.

"Lovers, lovers," yelled one of the Germans, hanging from a window and waving, barely visible through the wild spray of mud.

"Assholes!" screamed David.

Darcy was choking, spitting. Her breath came in gulps. Tears glistened in her eyes before turning dark on her cheeks.

They were both solid mud, poorly executed sculptures of wet clay. Once again David started to wipe the debris from Darcy's face. She pushed his hand away.

"Don't touch me," she cried, and stumbled from him.

They walked apart, side by side, silent except for an occasional stifled sob. When they got beyond the power plant, David stopped and slid the four sandals from his belt, slapping them together to knock off the worst of the clotted mud. The lights of Phira were no longer ahead but around them. Their feet made new grinding sounds on the coarse, chalky gravel. Square two-story stucco houses, blue and white and identical, slid one into the other on both sides of the street.

This end of town was asleep. Front gates were latched, shutters closed. A small pack of dogs took their pleasure in the deserted street. Now and then David raised his hand to wipe the sweat from his forehead or clean the scum that kept gathering at the corners of his mouth. Beside him, Darcy's small sobs gave way to sniffing.

Don't touch me, she had said. All right, fine, he wouldn't touch her. He didn't want to touch her. He just wanted to get her on the goddamn boat. I don't understand why I'm leaving, she had said. Well, this was one fine example of why. She gets dirty and it's my fault. All the goddamn time it's my fault. Who could live with that? At the end of the street, now lined with darkened shops, he could see the cobbled square.

The town square, lit up and awake. Even at this late hour there would be men there, huddled at small tables to discuss politics and paternity over tiny cups of Turkish coffee. If the *Oia* had arrived, there would be additional things to talk about, additional tables occupied. If. David walked faster.

To the square's left sat Santorini's mother church, squat and massive. To its right, the Hotel Nicolaos, whose lazy waiters served the tables. Straight ahead, nothing. Only the moon and a heavy iron rail to discourage the long fall to the sea below.

Table by table the Greeks abandoned their conversation as the couple entered the square, watching without statement as they wove their muddy way toward the open sky.

"It's here," said David softly, his stomach pressed to the rail.

Several hundred yards below, and a half kilometer out on the black sea, lay the *Oia*. Dominating the night, lit up like a small city, it made David's breath come hard. He studied the unwavering reflection on the water and decided it wasn't moving, was anchored. He looked for other lights, smaller moving lights that would be launches shuttling passengers and freight back and forth to the big ship, but could see nothing.

"Let's hurry," he said. Somewhere among the confused lights at the pier below there had to be one last boat waiting to ferry out late passengers. He grabbed Darcy's hand.

She jerked away from him, walked quickly on, toward the cathedral and the steps just beyond. David followed. In front of the church a bearded priest in black cassock and conical hat stood as though a shadow of himself. As Darcy and David passed before him, he slowly inscribed a cross in the night air. David raised his fist but didn't shake it as he had thought to do.

At the top of the steps the taxi driver lounged against the

railing, talking with two of the young donkey drivers. Half a dozen donkeys stood by, idle and smelly, their long sad heads hung nearly to the ground. Any other time David would have already been approached by one of the boys soliciting him to hire one of the animals, if not for himself or the luggage, at least for the comfort of the lady. But now they just grinned.

It didn't matter. David figured they could make better time on foot anyway. The taxi driver smiled broadly and took a deep, slow bow as they passed. David looked away. Darcy had started down the steps.

Carved directly into the cliff, the narrow stone steps zig-zagged their way to the bottom in a series of dizzying reversals. And, falling as directly as possible to the pier, they were unusually steep, always more than a foot high, sometimes two. More railing, old but unbroken, guarded the seaward side of the route.

"Faster," yelled David. "You've got to go faster."

"I can't. I'll slip." Darcy was still slightly ahead, but each step seemed to pose a greater task for her short legs, and with each step she hesitated longer. Her hand never left the rail.

Passing her, he took the lead. He would set the pace. Below he could make out the small dark shapes of men moving about on the pier, pushing and dragging other dark shapes.

Now and then they met a donkey, its back laden with bags of grain or suitcases, homecoming Greek or tourist. Indifferent to oncoming traffic, the animals kept to the middle of the path, forcing David and Darcy to the side. When one brushed against Darcy, she screamed. The donkey bolted ahead, a leather valise slid from its back and bounced on up the steps at the end of a rope.

"It tried to kick me," she cried.

"Are you hurt?"

"No."

"Then come on."

With each step the canvas bags slammed against his hips

and the straps dug deeper into his shoulders. He didn't stop when he heard one of the seams in the faded yellow bag give way, but unfastened his belt, slid it from his waist, and cinched it over the widening split. They were halfway down the steps when his mind was jarred by the sudden absence of a sound behind him. Darcy's footsteps. Turning around, he saw her sitting on a step, her body sagging forward and her head between her knees.

"What's wrong now, for chrissake?"

"My sandal, it broke."

"Take it off."

"The steps are covered with donkeyshit."

"No worse than mud."

"I have to rest."

"Move, goddammit."

"I'm afraid. I'll fall."

David started back up the steps, to drag her on if he had to, but she rose when she saw him coming. She steadied herself on the railing, pulled off the broken sandal, and flung it to the sea. She took a step down. Their dirty faces met, a foot apart.

"Why have you done this?" she said.

"I haven't done a thing. Your sandal broke, that's all. Would you say that was my fault, Darcy? Would you say that?"

He turned from her and was again rushing down the steps. He could see that one of the launches roped to the pier was being loaded with luggage and beside it, standing at the edge of the concrete where the black water rose and fell, he recognized the six well-dressed young men.

He was taking the steps as fast as he could. Several times he nearly slipped on the soft splotches of greasy excrement left behind by the donkeys. Darcy fell farther and farther behind, but it hardly mattered now; as long as he could reach the launch before it left, he could make it wait.

One by one the Germans were getting into the boat. As David climbed lower he could see puffs of white smoke rising from its back and realized that the inboard engine was already running. The third German, a bottle clasped to his breast, had to be helped into the launch. The fourth and fifth jumped from the pier at the same time, the boat rocked, their balance was lost. Like vaudevillians, they fell toward each other and embraced awkwardly, settling together on a wooden seat. A donkey loaded with crates started up the steps toward David. A boy ran alongside, beating its flanks with a stick.

Darcy had disappeared above, behind the last turn. David lost his footing and found himself sitting on cold damp stone. The last German climbed into the launch. On the pier an old Greek bent low to uncoil a line and tossed it to the floor of the boat. The donkey clambered past and the boy called out: "*Athio, athio, athio.*" Goodbye.

David got up and scrambled down the last few steps. The back of the launch pivoted from the pier, leaving a curved path of creamy froth on the black water. When it was pointed straight out to sea, the old man threw the other line and the boat slowly backed away from the platform.

"No. Wait. Don't go!" David ran from the bottom of the steps across the short pier, shouting and waving his arms above his head. It couldn't leave. Not now. The canvas straps slid toward his neck, burned into the bare damp flesh.

From behind and above, high and thin and wavering as he had never before heard it, Darcy's voice reached for him.

"Finish it, you coward. Finish it!"

He stopped. The concrete had ended. Thirty feet of sea and foam separated him from the launch, which for a moment was motionless as it reversed its engine.

"Coward!"

Again the boat was moving. Coming toward him, coming back. David let his breath spill out. It was going to be okay. But the boat was pulling by him, working its way through a wide arc, sliding by him, the bill of the pilot's cap pointed away, pointed out. Until the boat itself was moving away, its engine suddenly louder, its engine thrashing the water, moving away, out toward the *Oia*.

"Stop! Stop." The words were dead on David's lips. His

arms fell wooden at his sides. Unable to look away, he watched as one of the Germans stood up in the back of the launch and pointed toward shore.

"*Liebhaber*," he called out across the water, "*du bist ein* lover."

"Stop."

"Lover."

The other Germans joined the first, and as the launch moved farther and farther away, as its two small lights were swallowed by the lights of the *Oia*, the chant seemed to grow louder.

Lover. Lover. Lover.

Last Factory Blues

RIGHT FROM THE START I could see that Donny was bugged about something. Not that I'm especially interested in his problems, I mean I got enough of my own, right, but when I come on the shift he's standing there by the time clock with his card in his hand and his head up his butt and when Ferguson who's behind him tells him to get his fat ass in gear Donny doesn't say a word, not a word, just puts his time card back in his slot without punching it and walks off.

It was the same thing when I saw him in the john. I was pissed because there wasn't any Dixie cups and you can't take aspirin without water and I don't like shoving my head in the sink, and Donny's over there by his locker with this look on his face like he's just been shot and is waiting for the pain to start. Well he's as good a friend as I got on the job so I yell over to him, "Hey Donny, who pulled your plug?" Trying to be nice, you know, trying to make a little cheap conversation.

"Shove it," he says.

Alright fine, I think to myself, to hell with him. I got enough on my mind and he's right, I got no business taking on more, so I stick my head under the faucet and took my aspirin and went on out to the presses.

Chuck's already on his and unloading, though it isn't even starting time yet, and when I get to mine I see I got the same three molds I had the day before.

They were the same molds I'd had for a couple weeks now and I was getting to where I could make real fine time on them. That's the only way to your bonus and the only way to your sweet roll at Ontawa Rubber, to know your molds as well as you know your old lady's box.

So I got presses four, five, and six and Donny's right across from me on nine, ten, and eleven, except that for a change I was pulling molds before he was – I'd been down the line once before he even came out from the john.

On four I was pulling lens caps for Kodak, it was printed right on them so I know, on five I was using an air hose to pop out little nipples like you see on the end of eyedroppers, and on six I was making bootheels. Sometimes the heels stick to the plate if I don't use enough soap and then I have to pry them off with a piece of flat brass, but all in all it was a pretty easy line and I was getting it down cold.

Donny's molds, though, had been getting tougher lately. He's a hell of a big guy and I guess they figured he ought to be able to handle more. The day before, they gave him two of those mothers you're supposed to use a chain hoist just to open they're so heavy, but after he got mad he wouldn't use it, just opened them with his hands, slamming back those big lids against the press so that I thought sure he was going to break something, the mold or the press or maybe his back.

The super had been around and said to use the hoist but Donny told him to lay off, maybe if he had better molds he would be a little more careful. Well Donny's not the kind of guy you argue with if you got any brains at all so the super just shrugged and came over to give me some grief instead, said I was using too much soap and it would fuck up the plates. Bastard.

So at first I thought maybe that was what was bothering Donny today, getting such lousy mold assignments and not being able to make bonus. But when he finally came out from the john and got started I could see that they had given him pretty decent ones for a change. Like he had cap snafflers on ten and they really pay.

But he was still on the rag, and the way he was knocking things around I figured for sure he's going to get into it with the super again and this time there might be trouble.

But nothing happened and after a while Donny and I fell into sync like we usually do. Donny started right off hitting it hard, setting the pace, and the aspirin seemed to be doing a little more than usual, or maybe it was that by now I knew every trick and shortcut there was to know on my line of molds. At any rate I was staying right with him.

It's nice how that works, when you get the timing down. It's like music. Every press and every mold has its own kind of noise, then there is the banging of the tools and hiss of the air hoses and the sound of the soapy water hitting the hot plates and you get rhythms going, hard rhythms like in blues. Then *they* keep *you* going. You don't think about it.

Donny's right across from me, our machines are back to back, and when we're really on the money I can see him every time I raise a press. The timing has to be perfect though because there's only that one split second, when we both lift at the same time and there's that sudden open view. When we hit it's like being in a hotel room and opening your door just as the guy across the hall opens his. You can see right through and it's like you want to smile.

So we're moving hard down the line and have some good blues going, with Chuck getting in on it from over there next to Donny, but every time I'm up I have to look at Donny's sad fat face and there's no smile there, none at all.

Usually I don't think about much of anything while I'm on the job, which is one of the things I like about it, but if my back or joints get to bothering me I'll sometimes try to concentrate on something else — something, you know, positive. Like what I'm going to do when I get my sweet roll together. I've got more than a thousand in the bank now but I'm looking to double it, then it'll be goodbye Ohio and hello sunny Florida.

But instead I can't get my mind off Donny, wondering what it is that's bugging him, and I'm getting pissed at myself because whatever it is it's none of my business and I don't want it to be.

So at break I stayed away from him, waited until he was out of the john before I went in to take some more aspirin, and I waited until he was through at the Coke machine before I went over to get myself a Sprite. I didn't want to talk to him, didn't want to hear about it, so I wasn't ready when he comes up behind me and jumps me with that question.

"Hey, has your Linda ever insulted you, bad?"

"Like how?" I said, knowing the question was a mistake.

"Like called you a pig? Called you a fucking pig?"

"Nah."

In fact, my Linda would never say anything like that. We're not married so she's real careful. But Donny's Linda, I've seen her, she picks him up at twelve, and it wasn't too hard to picture her giving him shit.

"What would you do if she did, if she called you something like that?"

I knew exactly what I would do but I didn't say it, I didn't say anything. I was wishing I'd stayed in the john.

"Maybe I should have belted her," he said. But there he was wrong. Donny is a hell of a big guy, but she's big too. A real heavyweight. She'd probably have belted him back.

"You didn't punch your time card when you came on, Donny, did you know that?" I said, trying to change the subject.

He said I was full of shit but after a minute he headed over to the time clock to find out for sure. I was glad to be left alone. This time the aspirin wasn't doing a damn thing. My legs felt like concrete that's just being made, especially up high in my thighs, and my fingers felt like they'd been caught in a car door.

I took a couple more aspirin and wandered back out to the machines.

What had they been fighting about this time? I couldn't keep myself from thinking about it and I couldn't help but feel sorry for Donny, being stuck with a woman like her.

He's only been married about a year, which is about how long I've lived with my Linda, but when I first started working for Ontawa way back then Donny was sure a lot happier. They put him on my press with me at first, to show me the ropes, and he was real decent about it even though it cut into his bonus time. We never talked much, though, until I happened to mention my Linda's name.

"Same as my wife's," he said, and I remember this big grin on his face and him thumping me on the back like that made us brothers or something.

After that he would bend my ear every day about her, how she had fixed him a whole veal dinner — a lot of the guys just heat something up right on their press — or how she had made him a shirt, because it was hard for him to find anything big enough uptown, or how he had let her choose the color of the pickup they were going to buy and she had picked a terrible mustard yellow but it was what she wanted and wasn't that funny. I never said much but he didn't seem to mind that I wasn't real interested and I'm easy, a real sucker, so I listened.

For a while it seemed like he was telling me everything. Like how they had screwed three times the night before and in what positions, which was real hard for me to imagine, I mean, the two of them wrestling around must have really rocked that little trailer they live in. And how she had squealed when he brought her one of those porno books from the dirty bookstore downtown.

Then one day he tells me that she's going on a diet and wants him to also and what did I think? I told him I didn't have an opinion on that but it was a lie, if Donny lost fifty pounds he would still be overweight.

From then on things started going to hell for Donny. For a week she refused to do any housework, wouldn't make the bed or take out the garbage, nothing, until he promised her a color television set.

Then they started to argue about everything. They argued about where they should go on their vacation and had a fight over the kind of carpet they should get for the trailer and she started ragging him about why did he have to work the late shift and leave her alone nights? I mean they even fought about who should set the mousetrap and who should empty it. Jesus. He'd tell me all about it, then ask how it was going with my Linda, making it pretty obvious that what he wanted was advice.

Well I didn't have any so I would just say things were fine with us, I kept my foot down, although the truth of it was that I wasn't so sure how it was going with us. Not that we fought or anything, that would have been a relief. It was that we didn't fight.

She wouldn't get mad at me, even when I couldn't help but give her reason to, and if I got pissed at her it was tears, a few tears and her saying she understood and I was right and she was wrong and was sorry, really sorry, and please would I forgive her. Jesus. It got on my nerves, I don't know why.

Then there was this sex business. It was like she thought I should be ready to go any time day or night, even after work when sometimes it hurts just to take off my clothes.

"Don't you want me," she would say, "don't you want me? I want you." What she wanted was kids. I know. She never said it direct, but every time a friend of hers got married she would come back from the wedding all starry-eyed and for weeks afterwards she would be full of bright ideas about how we should move to a bigger place or should buy a new car together or would say crazy things like how she ought to stop taking the pill. It made me take more aspirin.

But I guess those weren't big problems compared to what Donny was going through.

After a while his Linda stopped cooking for him. She told him she wasn't going to work up a sweat over separate meals for him when she had to live on Jell-O and cottage cheese. She would fix him tuna fish and lettuce sandwiches for work, but no more than two, and told him he was selfish for even wanting more.

"What am I," he said one night, "a goddamned rabbit? You work, you got to eat."

He would bring TV dinners, heat them up on a press, and have them along with his sandwiches. Before work he would eat Italian down at Tony's and on his way home after work I know he usually stopped for a quick hamburger. But he wouldn't blame his Linda for any of it. She was getting better looking every day, he said. It was just that the diet made her irritable. The diet explained a lot of things, he said. The last time I saw her her hair was frosted and up in a bouffant, but she still looked like a wrestler to me.

So I'm thinking about all these things and trying not to as I work down the line, filling my baskets with lens caps and nipples and heels, when I realize I've fallen behind. Donny wasn't saying anything, but it had thrown off the blues and that's no good, so I picked it up.

I was a little better, those extra aspirin must have hit home, so it didn't take me long to catch up and we were in perfect sync again. Of course that also meant I was looking at Donny's miserable face every time we opened our presses, but this time I get to thinking about Florida and what it would be like heading ten or twenty miles out into the Atlantic every morning and we were just cruising, coming down on the supper break, halfway home. We were making good time and we all knew it.

About seven I put my jar of chili on my press without even breaking stride and by seven-thirty it was good and hot. You can't actually cook anything on the presses, just warm stuff up. It took Donny's TV dinners the whole four hours to get there and then sometimes they were still soggy, but that night when we shut down the presses I saw that he didn't have one at all, just his regular two sandwiches.

I took off my gloves and went to the john to wash my hands and while I'm in there I notice they still haven't got any paper cups. Jesus, you'd think the least they could do is make it easy for a man to get a drink of water.

Then I went back and got my chili and was already in the

dining hall when I realized I hadn't punched out for supper. So I had to get up and go do that, and goddamn if Donny's not hanging around the time clock like he wants to talk. Shit. The aspirin has been tearing up my stomach even though it's the buffered kind, and so I'm in a big hurry to get back to my chili because food always helps, and the last thing I want is a conversation. So when he opens his mouth to start talking I cut him off with something about how hot it is and why wasn't he eating himself. He was going to, he said, but I didn't wait around for him, just punched out fast and hustled back to the dining hall.

All I had was the chili so it didn't take me long to eat, though I eat fast no matter how much I got. A few of the guys are bitching about their molds and Chuck's into his thing about his car, cost him a hundred and sixty the day before, and that gets me back to thinking about my sweet roll.

I don't know when I'll have enough, but what I got in mind is hooking up with a couple old army buddies of mine down in the Florida Keys who already have a nice little fishing operation going and are looking for another partner. Mostly they just troll for king mackerel, good decent work in the open air. I mean, I know it's something I'd be good at.

Then the conversation drifts into women, like it always does, and that makes me think about Donny again, and I'm wondering where he is and why he isn't eating when suddenly he's sitting down next to me and unwrapping a tuna fish sandwich.

Bill Ferguson is telling a story about some sweet-mouthed cosmetologist down in Lima and what she did for him three times in one night, and old Marv Jacobs says he always did wonder what that word meant and was glad to find out even if it was too late to do him any good. But Frank Joad, who's a grandfather himself, says "Hell, you're never too old."

"Had a woman tell me once that she liked old men and fat men the best because they tried harder and appreciated it more."

Then Ferguson, who's a tough punk but dumb, says, "Hey

Donny, is that true? Do the ladies get all damp just waiting to climb up on your big belly?" Most of the time that would have got a laugh, even from Donny, but I could tell from Donny's face which was puffy and red, and the way he puts down his sandwich on the table, that this time what it's going to get Ferguson is trouble.

"Shut your hole, you slob," says Donny.

"Hey look who's calling who..." was as far as Ferguson got, I'm surprised he got that far, before Donny just reached across the table and punched him a good one on the ear. And it shut him up alright, although he still looked like he was ready to fight until Donny put up his hand showing it was over. I guess the others must have thought Ferguson had it coming too because they just started talking again so the kid wouldn't get much satisfaction out of pushing it any further.

Donny finished his sandwich and I didn't like it how quiet he was.

Then he was unwrapping his second when all of a sudden he turns to me and starts talking, low enough for the others not to hear but real fast, like the words were hot and he had to get rid of them quick.

"What I don't understand is why she is so hateful. I've never done a single thing to hurt her. Not a single thing. Even when she said she didn't want to sleep in the same bed with me anymore I said okay if that's the way you feel about it but I can't understand why you feel that way and you know what she tells me? She says it's because I drool on the pillow. God, I didn't know I drooled. Then she tells me her brother drooled on his pillow and she hated it that her folks made her sleep with him when she was little and she hated her brother and her brother was a fat fucking pig and so was I. God."

His face still looked swollen but it wasn't red anymore, it was pink like a baby's.

"Then she started yelling and screaming for me to get out, so I went down to Tony's and she had me so crazy that I got on the phone and called her father, at work for chrissake, in Cleveland, I get him out from underneath a car, and I ask him why she would act crazy like that had she ever gotten crazy like that before and he said no not that he could recall and then I ask him if she really hated her brother that much and he tells me that her brother died before he could walk, I should know that, so how could she hate him? God, why would she make something like that up?"

By the time he got to that his face was only about ten inches from mine and I could smell his sweaty T-shirt and his eyes were wide open and I could have sworn he wasn't breathing at all. He was waiting. I think he expected me to have an answer. Well I didn't, so I started looking in all my pockets for a match, not looking very hard if you know what I mean, and by the time I found one and got my cigarette lit he had let out his breath, long and slow and dead-smelling, like the air out of an overinflated tire, and I figured it was okay. I figured he just had to get that off his chest and now that he had he would be okay.

And I was right, I guess, because after that Donny went back to unwrapping his other sandwich and for the first time that day his face looked relaxed.

His Linda had really done a job on it. She had wrapped it so many separate times with Saran-wrap that even though Donny had already taken off five layers of the stuff you still couldn't see through to the bread. And if Donny thought that was a little strange you sure couldn't tell by watching him, peeling off those squares one by one and smoothing them out on the table like he was going to save them.

I couldn't understand his concentration and I couldn't keep from watching, even though I didn't want to. It must have taken him five minutes to get down to the sandwich itself and when he did, when he had finally finished, he just let it sit there on that last cellophane square, like that was it, the whole thing, unwrapping it.

Well Donny's not the sort of guy to let a sandwich go to waste so I'm sitting there, staring at the damn thing and getting nervous, I don't know why, because he won't pick it up. I figured it was tuna fish because he always had tuna fish, but of course I couldn't be sure, so I'm studying the edge of the bread just as he finally reaches out his hand and that's when I noticed it. A black thing hanging out the back of the sandwich, like a shoelace or something.

But I didn't say anything, just watched as he took a long slow bite and chewed for a while. My shoulders were aching and I was thinking about maybe taking a couple more aspirin now that I'd eaten, when I notice Donny carefully opening up the sandwich and looking inside and so am I, I can't help it, and there it is, I see it. A mouse. There's a goddamn mouse in that sandwich. Squashed down on the bread with its four legs pointing in four different directions and its teeth showing.

But Donny didn't say a word about it, not a word, just shut the sandwich back up and sat it down slowly on the table, on that last square of Saran-wrap. It made me wonder if he had even seen it, and he didn't let me know one way or the other, just sat there like a dead man, with his eyes fixed on that sign that hangs next to the door.

Pleeze
Lend a Hand!

Put You're
LITTER
in the Can!

Well I'm not the squeamish type but seeing that mouse with its flattened head was enough for me, so I got up off my ass and out of the lunch hall. I went to the Coke machine and got another Sprite and headed back out to the presses even though there was five or ten minutes of the supper break left.

Every muscle in my body was tight and I'm getting out four aspirin when that bastard supervisor comes over, wants to know what kind of pills I'm taking, like it's some goddamn business of his.

"How come there aren't any Dixie cups in the john?" I say.

"You got a bad heart or what?" he asks.

I got a heart that's shrinking, that's what, getting smaller and tighter and harder every day so that I'm worried it might just give up.

"It isn't asking for much, paper cups," I say.

"Asthma, you got asthma?"

I can't breathe but that's not the reason why. I can't breathe because the air in here is hot and thick like chicken soup and the air at home is no better, full of I'm sorry's and forgive me's, and I tell you I'm drowning in the air I breathe.

"Cups, for chrissake, how about some paper cups?"

"Poor circulation, hemorrhoids, hernia, insomnia, fatigue – what's bothering you, Jackson? You use too much soap on your plates."

Sure. I got all those things, but when I tell my Linda what does she say? Let's make love, you'll feel better. And when I tell my doctor? Nothing. He says there's nothing wrong with me. Tells me to eat right and get some sleep. Stop smoking.

"Your health is our concern," says the super. "You're going to break something." He is right, and whatever it is I can feel it starting to crack right now.

"Cups!" I yell into his face.

"Watch the soap!" he yells into mine.

And I know that if we go any further I will end up without a job. But just then Chuck comes over and says something about how his chain hoist isn't working right, is slipping, and the bastard walks off to look at it.

Sometimes I would like to punch guys like him but there are a lot of people I would like to punch, and I didn't want to think about that so I ran up four and pulled the mold. Every fucking bootheel was stuck to the plate, like they had been glued there, and it took me five minutes to pry them off. I gave the plate a good soaping after that.

I didn't have any mold problems from then on and I'd been hitting it good for fifteen minutes or so, working so hard that my mind had gone blank like I wanted, when Donny comes back on. And right away my brain is bouncing around like a pinball.

Where has he been, in the john? What did he do with that sandwich? What's he going to do about his Linda?

I try thinking about Florida and how that salt air will feel at five in the morning, but already he's caught up with me and we're in sync and every time my press is up there he is. And I swear to God he's staring at me, like there's something I can do to change things.

I try not to look back but I can't and after a while I'm seeing just his lips and wondering if he really does drool on his pillow. Then somehow that gets me thinking about my Linda's knuckles and how they crack. All the goddamn time they crack. When we're in bed it drives me nuts.

Donny had picked up the pace and I was staying with him, even though it was knocking me out and even though I wouldn't have had to look at him if I'd just dropped back a little. But we had some good fast blues going, as fast as I can ever remember, and I couldn't bring myself to break them.

And it didn't seem to matter anymore what I was thinking because it was all getting kind of crazy like when you're at a party where everyone's drunk and things are spinning and there's no point in worrying or trying to make things stop.

When I heard the ten-o'clock whistle I didn't even finish unloading five, just dropped the air hose and headed for the Coke machine. My shirt was soaked and I could barely straighten my neck, but all I was thinking about was two more hours, two more hours and I can go home.

I got my Sprite and sat down and had taken a couple more aspirin when Chuck comes up behind me and asks what was going on with Donny out there, he was busting his fat ass, and when I turned around I saw that Donny hadn't even slowed down, was working right though the break.

I said I didn't know and I didn't really give a shit and then I must have closed my eyes because the next thing I know Chuck's poking me in the ribs saying let's go, break's over.

I didn't even try to keep up with Donny anymore. I just set a good steady pace for myself and stuck with it. Every once in a while Donny and I would happen to be up at the same time and I would look through at him, but his eyes were dead, like the eyes of a fish that's been cooked, and I don't think he even noticed me staring at him.

And Donny didn't stop, didn't even slow down, when Chuck's chain hoist broke and the lid of his mold on twelve came down on his fingers. He had jerked back pretty good when the chain snapped, so it was only the tips of a couple of fingers, but when I got around there and saw the Ferguson kid peeling back the bloody glove, I knew Chuck was off the job. The lid had done real neat work, bitten them off right at the first knuckle, and Chuck was just standing there with this "what happened" look on his face.

Then the super comes over and tells Ferguson and I to get back to work, he would take care of it, and told Chuck to come with him up front. You could have tracked them by the trail of red on the floor, like paint.

There was only about half an hour to go in the shift after that and I didn't feel like working anymore at all but there was nothing I could do for Chuck and I didn't want to talk to Ferguson so finally I went back to my presses with the idea that I would just sort of take it easy, coast. And I'd been down the line once, real slow, and was pulling lens caps on four when I realized that Chuck's machines were still going.

I couldn't see them but I could hear them, the hissing of the steam as they went up and down, the heavy scrape of the molds going in and out, the bang-slamming of the lids, back against the press, then down and shut hard. And they were going a lot faster than Chuck ever worked them.

I left the lens caps and went around to see what the hell was going on.

There was Donny on twelve, pulling the mold that got

Chuck's fingers, jerking up the heavy lid like it was made of cardboard. He unloaded it, bottle caps or maybe they were radio knobs, I don't know, threw in some rubber stock, dropped the lid, and had the mother back in that press right now. Then he moved on to thirteen, sweat dripping off his nose, without looking up, without so much as a sneeze in between.

"He's gone bongo," said Ferguson, who was leaning against the wall and smoking a cigarette, watching. "He's running all six of them, doesn't know what he's doing."

I didn't say anything, just watched poor Donny making time on Chuck's machines, the extra flesh on his arms and chest shaking like a fat woman's ass as he pulled and pushed and pounded out those last factory blues.

"Look at the fat fucker go!" Ferguson yelled, his hands cupped at his mouth. Then in a more confidential voice he says to me, "I could have predicted this. I'd of nailed him back at supper except I could tell he was going nuts. It ain't right to hit a crazy man."

Donny was moving faster and faster.

He cracked the lid of one mold but just kept going like it didn't matter, like it wasn't worth the five hundred bucks it cost anyway.

Another one hadn't been in the press long enough and the rubber was still sticky so he just ripped the product out with a screwdriver. That must have scratched the plate real good.

"Here comes trouble," says Ferguson and it's the super he's talking about, moving as fast as I've ever seen the bastard move. And there's not a single part of my body that's not sore.

Ferguson must have thought he was coming for us because we weren't working, but he was going for Donny, and I'm thinking I'll probably have to take some more aspirin.

Donny's on eleven and when the super gets there, Donny doesn't even look up. Just reaches across the bench and picks up a crowbar and when the super starts to say something he spins around and comes up with it between the bastard's legs, catching him a solid one in the nuts.

And maybe it's crazy but I'm thinking about knuckles,

Chuck's knuckles, my Linda's knuckles, cracking, and the super is on the floor and screaming like a baby and Donny's moved on to twelve, the one that got Chuck, like nothing's happened, like nothing's happened at all.

And me, I'm leaving. I'm going to the time clock and punching out and I know I'm only coming back to pick up my check. And I know I'm not going home to Linda tonight, but I'll go over there in the morning, while she's at work, and get my things, and I'm thinking about Florida.

My Journal as the Fishwoman

BEFORE I EVEN START, let's get one thing straight. This whole dumb thing is Dublonsky's idea, not mine. When he suggested it, last Wednesday, I had to laugh.

"I'm not trying to be funny," he said, even though he himself was grinning and all the time leaning forward out of his chair, trying to bait me with that big, tooth-sparkling Robert Redford smile of his. For fun I decided to play along.

"A journal?" I said. "What would I write about?"

"About yourself," he said.

"But where would I start?" I asked.

"At the beginning, Jenny. Start at the very beginning."

That's a shrink for you.

o

The beginning? I can't remember, of course, but my mother says I had it, it was there, right from the first moment she laid eyes on me. She says my bottom was pinker than those of other babies, and it was the wrong kind of pink. More like red, burnt.

At first the doctors weren't concerned and told my mother she shouldn't be either. I was healthy, they said. An unusually bad case of diaper rash, yes, but healthy. Nothing to worry about. It would go away. They recommended ointments and salves that could be bought over the counter.

It didn't go away, it spread. This is the way my mother

tells it: like a smoldering fire it crept up my dimpled back and down my fat little legs, claiming one dark red handful of me after another. Pausing from time to time but never retreating, it slowly moved over my body, consuming my flesh like so much firewood until it reached my ankles and wrists and neck. Then, there, out of some perverse last-minute kindness, it stopped. I was two by then and my mother was twenty-two. And she was alone. She says my father never came back from Vietnam, but I know better. He came back, looked at me one time, and split. He couldn't handle my disease.

Oh, my mother suffered with me, there's no doubt about that. Because of me, Dublonsky would like to say.

I know this, too: when it became apparent that the doctors had no answers, and for that very reason were extremely interested in my body, she bundled me up and brought me across New York City by bus to this place, the Downstate Medical Research Center. Here, I imagine her saying to the resident dermatologists, take my child. My daughter. Please. I imagine tears, too, but of course I can't be sure.

Papers were signed, I have seen them. With certain conditions, they took me. It's sad, but my earliest memories of adults are not of my parents at all but of doctors and nurses, especially nurses, all in starched white.

o

Yesterday was Wednesday again. Dublonsky and I had our little session. I told him I had started on the journal, and I felt so good about it I almost winked at him.

"Wonderful," he said. "How much did you get written?"

"Only a couple of pages," I admitted.

"That's fine. More would be unhealthy. Where did you begin?"

"At the bottom," I said. "With my burnt little bottom."

He laughed at that, just like I knew he would. He thought I was being cute just for him. He thinks he sees through me.

"But I don't like it," I said. "I'm going to start over."

"That's fine," he smiled. "With something like this there

are always a great many beginnings; the important thing is that you've begun. What have you learned so far?"

Dublonsky is always at his charming best when he thinks he is leading a patient down the golden road of self-discovery. It makes me want to kiss him. So I couldn't resist telling him a truth I knew would excite him.

"I've learned," I said, "that I hate my mother."

o

I'm sitting outside, in the garden.

Starting over.

I don't want to talk about the past. I don't want to think about my mother. I'm beginning again, here, in the present.

I'm sitting outside in the garden. Me, Jennifer Voit, no middle name that I know of, twenty years old, sitting here in the flesh, because of my flesh, here under the sun according to doctor's orders, my back sticky against the canvas of this chair. Forty-nine-cent notebook on my lap, "My Journal" printed on its cover. Large paper cup full of crushed ice and Pepsi on this little table beside me.

It's late summer. I'm wearing a bikini, a very skimpy little blue thing, so that the sun has maximum access to me. The sun is my treatment.

I don't know why they bother to call this a garden. It's all concrete except for the tiny patch of grass in the middle and five undernourished shrubs growing up out of five square concrete planters. The water fountain doesn't work. And if I want to see the sky I have to look straight up — I'm surrounded by four brick hospital walls.

I'm not alone out here; I share the sun with three other patients. Two are old women sitting stiffly on a single concrete bench as if they're waiting together for a bus. With their splotchy, look-alike skin they could be sisters. The other is that guy Owen, whose last name I don't know and don't want to. He's sitting across the grass with his shirt off, reading some cheap men's magazine, the kind that is filled with naked women. And every so often I catch him looking over at me.

No, more than just looking. Staring, the jerk. He's been here all summer and been looking at me like that all summer.

I've mentioned it to Dublonsky. Dublonsky says I'm just being paranoid because of my skin. I tell him this guy Owen is looking at more than just my skin.

Besides, he's got skin problems of his own. Every time I run into him in the hall, and it's hard not to because his room is just two down from mine, I have to hear all about it. All about his dumb tattoos.

"Listen," he says, and explains again how they are, by slow degrees, being sanded off.

"Look," he says, and I have to watch as he peels back a bandage to expose a new smooth scar over a faint blue outline.

"You see what it is?" he says. What it was, he means. Each time it's a different scar and a different outline and I'm supposed to guess what it was. I say I don't care but that doesn't stop him from telling me.

"A beautiful naked island girl under a coconut tree," he explained last time. It was on his left arm, his bicep.

"That's dirty," I said.

"No it isn't. Look closer. See how her hands cover her, you know, private parts?"

"Well then, how sweet," I said. I just wanted to get away from him.

"Oh yeah, sweet, that's exactly right. Underneath her dancing, see, there is this lettering that says 'Saving Myself for You.'" He pointed.

"But not anymore, huh?"

I had to laugh.

His face dropped. "No, not anymore."

Then he said, "It's kind of sad, you know. When I made this muscle I could make her dance, just like she was alive."

o

Dublonsky is sure to ask me what I've been writing about when I see him at our next meeting. "Well, how's it going, love?" he'll say and give me one of his special conspiratorial smiles.

"It's not," I suppose I could tell him. "It's not going at all. I started out writing about myself in the garden and ended up writing about that jerk Owen in the hall."

But then, of course, he would want to investigate my feelings for the man. "What about his interest in you do you find most upsetting?" Or, "Why haven't you just come out and asked him why he looks at you the way he does?"

Dublonsky enjoys his work, that's obvious. Six short hours a day, four days a week, a fat salary talking to people he thinks should have problems. Asking clever questions. Studying reactions he himself has forced. An ideal job for someone who so enjoys his time off, playing tennis, skiing, sailing; each Wednesday I find myself staring at all the photographs of him that hang on his office wall.

Most of all I find myself staring at the picture of him standing on the deck of his sailboat, his eyes off in the distance, a huge red sun setting on the sea behind him. Him and the sun, that's what I see. Jesus.

But if I didn't also enjoy watching him do his job, leaning forward or back in quick, feigned interest, wearing one of his tight-fitting polo shirts, a little alligator or penguin or umbrella floating on his athletic chest like a seal of approval, I probably would have told him off a long time ago. Told him to go to hell with his professional prodding and well-mannered meddling. But instead I look forward to our little sessions. I admit it. And to make them more interesting, I provoke him with selected truths.

So when he asks me on Wednesday what I've been writing about, I won't mention that jerk Owen at all. I'll say, "Dublonsky, I've been writing about you."

o

When the dermatologists told me a year ago that I was going to begin seeing a shrink, I said like hell I was. They got stuffy and said like hell I wasn't, it was part of the new treatment. Take it or leave the Medical Center.

"All I ever hear about are new treatments," I screamed at Dublonsky that first Wednesday afternoon. "You know, I've just about had it with this goddamn place and your goddamn new treatments."

"Now, Miss Voit. The only thing people here want is to help you."

"Help me, shit. All they want to do is poke and scrape at my skin. And what the hell has psychiatry got to do with dermatology anyway?"

"There's still a lot we don't understand in the field of medicine, Miss Voit."

"That's for goddamn sure."

"Maybe our sessions will lead to something, maybe not. We'll be doing some studies. Meanwhile, you're my patient and I'm your doctor and you'll be seeing me once a week. Is that clear?"

"You're not my anything unless I accept you."

"Do you accept your skin?"

"I'm stuck with my skin."

"And you're stuck with me until I say otherwise. Is that understood?"

Oh, I hated him back then and told him so. I told him he was being a prick, a real professional prick, and when he appeared genuinely hurt by my words, I was glad.

"I refuse to call you Doctor," I said.

"All right, Jenny."

"You're just Dublonsky to me."

"Whatever you say, Jenny."

Now, of course, I would gladly call him anything he wanted. At night, alone with my imagination beneath hospital linen, I call him darling. But he is content with Dublonsky, and his content is my sadness.

o

Staring, that guy Owen will not stop staring at me. Every time I look up from my notebook there he is, peering at me over the top of his cheap, skin-filled magazine, his eyes full of nasty blue perversions. I've put on my sunglasses.

I've watched him in the halls. It's easy to see that he's dangerous. He moves slowly and cautiously, like the jungle animals I've seen on television. But the nurses, stupid cows that they are, they seem to think that he's the game and they're the hunters. I have to laugh, the way they gather to talk about him, the way they watch him. If they weren't so dumb, I would feel sorry for them.

Damn, he sees me looking back at him. He's getting up. Bare chest, bandages, and tattoos, coming my way. I wonder if he realizes I am writing about him. There's only one thing to do. I'll get up and be gone before he ever reaches my melted ice and warm Pepsi.

o

Today was Wednesday. Dublonsky was fifteen minutes late for our session. He seemed distracted, not at all his usual self, and he didn't even ask me about the journal. I was hurt. I mean after all this whole goddamn thing was his idea, wasn't it? But I didn't say anything.

"I've been thinking," he said after five minutes of silence.

"Yes?"

"About your adolescence."

"Pimples!" I said.

"Unhappiness?" he asked.

"Of course," I said, "pimples on my face and unhappiness every place else." It was true and not true. Actually I didn't have much of an acne problem; what I had was a skin problem.

"What about boys?" he said.

"Why were you late today?" I asked.

"Lousy service in the cafeteria." Lousy service my ass. I know he was with a woman, probably one of the nurses.

"If they looked hard, they never looked twice," I said.

"Encounters in the dark?"

"Never."

"Did you ever, do you ever..."

"Masturbate?" I said.

"Yes."

"Only with my right hand," I said. I was looking at his photographs on the wall.

"Tell me about your fantasies," he said.

I went quiet. I stayed quiet. I knew he was covering up, trying to hide something by making me talk, and I wasn't going to stand for it. Besides, I didn't feel like sharing those visions of myself as siren and mermaid, visions in which my scaly skin somehow became an advantage.

"When are you going on vacation?" I asked.

"Two weeks," he said. "How did you know?"

"Will you be gone long?" I wasn't about to tell him how I knew. The nurses don't think I have ears, and I don't want them to learn that I do.

"A month," he finally said.

I had hit upon it, his distraction. His eyes were suddenly stuck on my favorite photograph, of him and his sailboat, and I could tell that he had nearly forgotten about me.

"Going alone?" I asked.

He wouldn't answer. The silence was unbearable.

"Oh Jesus," I said, "sailing to Haiti," giving away more of my overheard news. "The sun is really bright down there, isn't it?" I couldn't help it. Not only would I miss him and be jealous of whoever he was taking, I would be jealous of all that incredibly healthy sun.

"Bright, but hot," he said.

I couldn't help myself. "I would love it," I said.

We were lost to each other, in our own worlds; his without a cloud and mine miserably overcast. We were quiet. Dublonsky fumbled, yes fumbled, for a cigarette. He knew he was playing his professional role poorly. Sometimes I imagine that he is the patient and I am the doctor, the way he can become flustered, the way he can be so easily manipulated.

"Adolescence," he said after a long and awkward minute, "is always difficult."

o

Even in the winter – when blue jeans and long-sleeved high-collared blouses hid my blistered skin from the eyes of others, made me appear to those who didn't know me like any other pretty teenaged girl in casual dress – my dreadful body was never far from my mind.

Winter meant that spring was coming, and spring meant my annual humiliation. It meant that the sun would begin to work its irony on me, would begin to dry and heal my already burnt skin, and the doctors at the Center would order me to bare my arms and legs. Jesus, how I dreaded those warm sunny days that brought the others at school together in dizzy romance.

Naked before my classmates, I would watch with them as the purple turned to red, then salmon, then white. And while they eagerly groped for each other's bodies in the halls and cafeteria and schoolyard, I would go to the bathroom and pick compulsively at the dry scales that formed on my own flesh. To my face the others were quiet, and maybe they were even a little afraid, because I was tough for a girl; but behind my back, I know, they called me the fishwoman.

I did well in school. I have a good mind, lousy compensation for my bad skin. And I worked harder than I needed to, secretly believing for a long time that I might be able to learn my way out of my condition.

My mind won me the highest marks in biology and chemistry, even made me valedictorian; but it never got me a boyfriend.

o

I'm in my room. It's midnight or later. I'm thinking about the fact that I will see Dublonsky only once more before his vacation. I'm feeling sad about it, sentimental, as though it might be our last meeting.

I'm thinking of the sea and all that sun; I'm thinking about Dublonsky and me together. I can't help it. Together in his photograph, on the deck of his boat, somewhere in the Caribbean. Just off the white pebbly shore of a little coconut-tree island. Maybe we've just been swimming.

"Dublonsky?" I say.

"Yes, Jenny?"

"Will it always be the same between us?"

"Of course, Jenny."

We're lying on the deck, naked, the sun beating down on our skin.

"Did you like it when we did it in the water?" I ask.

"I loved it," he says.

The sea is slap-slapping at the side of the boat. His hand is on my bottom, which is bronzed by the sun.

"Dublonsky?" I say.

"Yes, love?"

"Kiss me."

He kisses me. "Like this?"

"Like that," I say, "yes."

○

"No," I tell him.

That jerk, Owen, in the hall this morning.

"Not even once?" he repeats for the second time.

"Not even once," I say.

"If you don't have them bad they can almost be fun," he says. "At least at first."

He is disgusting me and he knows it. He is making me sick to my stomach and making me hate him even more than I already do, but he won't let me go.

"You can pick them up with your nails," he says, "and if you look real close you can see that they look just like what they call them. Little tiny crabs." One of his hands is in front of my face, and he is wriggling all of his fingers.

"You're crazy," I say. "Leave me alone."

"Of course if you don't get rid of them they get worse, and if they get bad enough they chew up your skin, make it raw."

"Don't talk to me about skin," I say.

"That girl down the hall, the one with the big birthmark on her face, she's got them. She told me."

"Let me go, goddammit."

"Okay, okay, don't get all worked up. I just thought you might be interested, that's all. Crabs are actually kind of interesting. If you'd ever had them you'd know what I mean."

"I've never had them," I say.

"I know." He was grinning with all his teeth, like something was terrifically funny.

"I'll *never* have them," I say.

He was laughing. "Don't be so sure, even the best people get them. One day you just start itching and then on about the third day you discover them."

"You're a jerk," I hissed in his face.

"Some of them are white and some of them are black but they all wriggle when you get them under your fingernail."

"Stop it!" I screamed as loud as I could; and, just as I expected, one of the nurses came running in her soft-soled nurse's shoes all the way down the hall. Squeak, squeak, squeak, her front flapping and her cute little nurse's cap bouncing and her shoes suck-sucking at the floor until she saw it was Owen and stopped short, panting.

"Oh," she says, and opened her mouth wide as if to say something more but I could tell nothing more was going to come out.

"No problem," says Owen, "no problem. I was just explaining crabs to Jenny here."

What cows these nurses are. "Oh," she says again, and turns her big dumb eyes on me — and what I saw there amazed me. I think she was jealous, jealous of me, for having been the lucky one to hear about Owen's social disease.

o

What I have is eczema.

Eczematoid dermatitis, my chart at the nurse's station says, which is just another way of saying Bad Skin.

When I was younger and more determined to understand

myself, I looked it up in a medical encyclopedia. "A chronic skin eruption of unknown etiology," it said, "marked by the presence of reddish patches ranging in size from a few centimeters in diameter to large plaques the size of the palm or larger." Oh Jesus, if they had only seen me in the spring.

The entry ran on for several pages, describing the silvery scales that sometimes occur and the areas most often affected. There wasn't much for me to learn. I was the fishwoman; they didn't know why. They suspected climate and weather, toxins and irritants that refused to be named. They were looking into allergens and fungi and diet and wondered about chemical imbalance. I hated them for their ignorance.

At the end there was a single paragraph on the treatments indicated. Ultraviolet light ("ordinary sunlight is best") and baths ("warm, frequent, and regular"). Sun and water, it was all they knew. Sun and water. I have been moving back and forth, from one to the other, all of my life.

Today, for instance, I had a bath just before noon, spent the afternoon in the garden, and now I've just had another bath. I'm sitting on my bed, naked to the air, drying. I can see myself in the mirror across the room.

It is only my disease that keeps me from being a good-looking woman, and this time of the year is the worst because my skin is actually at its best; pink, that's all, pink and slightly rough to the touch. So close to normal. In a dull light you would hardly notice the million pinpoints of red.

I wear my hair down to my breasts. My eyes are a deep blue, my eyelashes long. My weight is correct for my height, and I know its distribution is right, too. I polish my toenails.

When I was younger the injustice of it drove me crazy. I would have preferred, then, to have been wholly deformed, a freak, a circus sideshow. "Step right up, ladies and gentlemen, this may be your last chance ever to see the world's only medical mermaid, the Fabulous Fishwoman." I might have found some solace in that, some consolation in the crowd's attention. Instead I simply felt cheated, pathetically imperfect, and at night I clawed in anger and frustration at my pink flesh. Naturally it made my condition worse.

○

Dublonsky is a louse; I knew it all along.

Yesterday was Wednesday, our last meeting before his vacation. At first he was all smiles and so was I. I had already decided to level with him.

"I wish I was going with you," I said.

"Of course," he said, "it's a nice part of the world to visit."

"No, I mean I wish I was going *with you*."

"I'll send you a postcard," he said. "How's the journal coming?"

He was obviously determined not to hear me. It made me mad; I mean he's my psychiatrist and it's his job to listen to anything I have to say, right? Especially if it has to do with my emotions.

"I've stopped writing in it," I lied.

"That's too bad, Jenny."

"Maybe," I said.

"Why did you stop?"

"It was boring."

"You find yourself boring?"

"The other people, the other people I was writing about were boring."

"Like who?"

"Like you, Dublonsky. Writing about you was boring."

He gave me one of his cute little hurt looks then, one of his pretty professional pouts.

"Well, I'm sorry to hear that," he said, "but maybe it's just as well. I've been thinking. Perhaps it's time for us to discontinue our sessions. It's been a year now and we don't seem to have made any headway, would you agree?"

"I never wanted them in the first place, if you remember."

"I know," he said. "And maybe you were right. And maybe we should officially discontinue them now."

I was quiet. I was hurt. I suppose it showed. How could he do this, after all we had shared, all we had been through together? I felt a wetness at my eyes that I refused to let become tears.

"You're just like all the others," I said.

"What do you mean, Jenny?"

"You don't give a damn about me."

"You're being a child, Jenny."

I tasted salt water. I wanted to hurt him; I wanted to get my nails into his blue eyes and blond hair and dark, tanned flesh.

"I'm not a child," I said. "I am twenty years old."

"There's no reason for you to see me anymore."

"I'm a twenty-year-old woman," I said.

"You were right in the first place, Jenny, psychiatry doesn't have a thing to do with dermatology."

"How old does a woman have to be for you, Dublonsky?"

"I can't help you."

I was beside myself with anger. I would have spit at him, but I was choking into my hand. He offered me a Kleenex. I pushed it away. He wasn't even looking at me, he was staring at that stupid photograph of him and his sailboat on the wall.

I stood up. I stood in his line of vision. "You detest me," I said, "because I'm deformed. Admit it. You detest me because I have this hideous skin disease."

"It's not your skin that's the problem, Jenny."

"Then what is it?" I wanted to kill him. Then I would kill myself. "Just what is the goddamn problem?"

"Hate, Jenny. It's eating you up. You even hate yourself."

"Go to hell," I said.

"It'll be hot enough in Haiti," he said, the funny bastard.

I left then, stomped out of his office. I won't go back. I don't have to take that kind of crap from a lousy shrink who thinks he's a comedian.

o

Owen's last name is Bacon, can you imagine that? When I heard it – overheard, I should say, from the nurses – I had to laugh. Imagine having a name like that. Anyway, this guy Owen Bacon will not leave me alone. This afternoon, in the garden, it was more of the same and the worst yet.

"Listen," he said, coming up to where I was sitting before I even saw him, "I'm sorry for upsetting you the other day, with the crabs I mean."

"Look," I told him, "it's all right. Just leave me alone. Can't you see I don't want to talk to you?" I put on my sunglasses then, to show him I meant it.

"Yeah, I can see that," he says. "I know what you think of me."

"Well then?"

"I thought I would apologize anyway."

"Okay," I said, "you've apologized. Now will you please leave me alone?" I was trying to be nice.

"Don't worry," he says, "I'll be leaving soon enough for good." The way he said it, it was like it made him kind of sad. "By this time next week," he said, "I'll be on my way back to Arizona. My last tattoo comes off tomorrow, the very last one. Want to see it before it's gone?"

"No," I say, "I do not want to see it."

But before I know what is happening, before I can say anything more or do anything or even shut my eyes, he has undone the cord of his white hospital pants and turned around and let them drop and I'm face to face with his bottom and the message there in tiny purple lettering inside the outline of a heart.

If you want my heart just ask
Cause baby its feelin real fine
But dont ever ask
For my well traveled ass
Cause baby thatll always be mine

"What do you think?" he says.
"I think you put it in the right place," I said.
"Made it up myself."

I'm about to tell him what he can do now, where he can go, when out of the corner of my eye I notice the two old spotted ladies on the bench. They've forgotten all about their bus and they're staring goggle-eyed at Owen's bare ass and I know what's going to happen next. They're going to scream.

I wait for the nurses.

o

Nurses. They're all the same. They start out in the profession with their dumb little-girl ideas of helping mankind, and after a year on the floor end up with the much more convenient notion of just helping themselves to a man. Doctors, patients, visitors: I've watched them reach for every kind of guy that makes his way down these not-so-antiseptic halls. When I was thirteen I discovered one of them in the linen closet with the boy who delivered clean sheets. Last year it was the head nurse and the hospital administrator in the instrument room. Jesus.

In twenty years I haven't met a nurse I had any respect for.

But it's not so much the way they act around men that I hate; it's the way they act around me. Bouncing into my room every morning with sweet, idiotic smiles on their faces and saying, "Well, Jenny, how's our skin today." Our skin. Jesus.

When I was younger I sincerely wished that eczema was contagious.

Dublonsky and I were both right about one thing. There never was any real reason for me to be seeing him. In fact, there's no real reason for me to be in this hospital at all. My skin is the same this year as it was last year, and the only things I do for it that help are the same things I've always done: sun and water, water and sun. I don't need a hospital for that.

But they keep me here, let me stay, so they can mess with my body on the side. Vitamin shots, mineral baths, citric salves and steroid creams, the tests and experiments and studies never end.

Maybe they're afraid to dismiss me because I know too much. Or maybe they just can't figure out what they would do with all my medical records if I was gone.

But the reason I don't just leave on my own — the reason I've never considered it for more than five minutes — is simple. I don't know where I would go.

o

"Arizona," says Owen Bacon, "that's where all the action is these days. Lots of building going on there, Jenny, lots of good clean construction work. Tucson is a boom city."

This was last night and he was buying me a Pepsi in the cafeteria. The only reason I agreed to talk with him was to make the nurses jealous.

"I hate cowboys," I say.

"You've never seen a cowboy," he says. "And it'll be a great bus ride down too, across Texas. You've never seen the sun shine till you've seen it shine in north Texas. Of course it'll be a little dusty."

"You've never *seen* a cowboy," he says. "And it'll be a great bus ride down too, across Texas. You've never seen the sun shine till you've seen it shine in north Texas. Of course it'll be a little dusty."

"I hate dust," I say.

"Yeah, me too, but the thing about north Texas dust is that it feels so good when you wash it off. Know what I mean?"

"No," I say.

"That's too bad, Jenny. That's a damn shame. Everybody ought to know what it feels like to wash the dust off."

He gets up then and goes to pay for our Pepsis, and when he's at the cash register I can see the bulge in his hospital pants, in the back, where his last tattoo has been sanded off and there's a big bandage over the raw skin.

"Yeah," he says when he gets back, "only five more days now and I'll be on that old Greyhound bus to Tucson."

"I hate buses," I tell him, "all you can do is sit there,

getting all cramped, and look out the window."

"Well then," he says with that big smile that exhibits all his teeth, "how about going for a little walk instead?"

I start to tell him how I hate going for walks – everyone stares at me – but before I can say anything he is already reaching out for me, grabbing my hands, pulling me to my feet, and all the people in the cafeteria, especially the nurses, are staring at us, I know they are.

o

I've been thinking about my mother today. When I was little she used to come visit me, but it was always terrible, a lot of stupid tears and crying, which nobody liked, so finally she moved to Florida with some real-estate man.

I remember the last time she came to see me. I was twelve or thirteen, and it was springtime. My skin was at its worst. I was in bed and they had my hands in cotton mittens, tied to the side rails so I couldn't dig at myself in my sleep.

"Jenny, my God, what have they done to you?"

Her crying awakened me. "They're torturing me, Momma," I said. "Untie me, untie me."

She untied me, I took off the mittens, and by the time the doctors and nurses heard her screams and got to the room, my sheets were gloriously soaked with blood. I had to laugh.

o

Owen and I have been going for walks every evening now. At least he's somebody to talk to. Even though I still hate him, I've decided he isn't such a bad person to talk to. Besides, he's only got two days left here at the Center.

Last night we walked around and around the block until we were tired, and then we went to the garden and sat on the bench where the spotted old ladies usually sit. It was getting dark and a little cold by then. Owen was telling me about how it stays warm in Tucson all year round.

It's strange how he has to sit, all sort of hunched forward

so that he's not sitting on that bandage. "Won't you be uncomfortable," I asked, "sitting like that all the way on the bus?"

"Sure," he said, "but it'll be worth it, it'll be worth it."

Then I asked him some other things I wanted to know.

"Where did you get them?"

"Get what?"

"The tattoos?"

"Here and there," he said. "Mostly in the Navy, but lots of different places actually."

"Why? Why did you get them?"

"Well now. I got some because I was happy, like when we laid over in the Marquesas Islands and me with that native girl, and some I got 'cause I was sad, like when my old mom died. One I got 'cause I didn't catch anything bad in Nam. Another 'cause I was head over heels, you know, in love with a girl from Bethesda, Maryland. But mostly I got them just for something to do."

"And you liked them?"

"Of course I liked them. I wouldn't have kept getting them unless I liked them."

"Then why are you having them all removed?"

He went real quiet then, like he'd been caught in some kind of trap, and I suddenly felt cold and my skin felt itchy and if he hadn't been sitting there beside me, I would have dug into myself with my nails.

"I mean, it must be very painful getting them off," I said. "Nobody would do that without a real good reason."

He was quiet for a long time, thinking over what to say, I guess, and when he was done he gave me a big white smile like he had decided something important, and he put his arm around my shoulder.

"Well now," he said, "I'll tell you but you have to promise me not to laugh."

"I won't," I said.

"It might sound kind of dumb."

I told him he shouldn't be so sensitive.

"Okay," he said. "The reason I got them off is because

tattoos always make you look and feel tough, and I was tired of being a tough guy."

I had to laugh. It was the dumbest thing I'd ever heard. Of course when he pulled his arm away and I looked at his face and saw the hurt there, I felt bad. Imagine, a grown man crying like that.

And I stopped laughing, but it was too late. He had already gotten up from the bench and started away from me.

"I'm sorry," I yelled, "really I am."

I ran after him but he wouldn't say anything more, wouldn't stop, and when I grabbed hold of his arm he pushed me away. I followed him all the way to his room but it didn't do any good, and when he slammed the door in my face I couldn't help it anymore, I started to cry myself.

o

I got a postcard from Dublonsky today. Black native girls with baskets on their heads and wearing a lot of stupid jewelry. The message on the back really didn't say anything at all. I threw it in the wastebasket, which is where I think this dumb journal also belongs.

o

This last part is Owen's idea. He says I shouldn't throw it away. He says that anything worth starting is worth finishing, and I guess he ought to know.

He's read everything else in here and knows all about Dublonsky, and he says that if I write down this last part I will feel better about the way things have turned out.

I feel better already. I started feeling better yesterday, in the afternoon, when I found Owen in the cafeteria and he accepted my apology almost as though nothing bad had happened between us at all.

"It's okay," he said, "I was just being sensitive like you said I shouldn't be."

"I cried all night," I told him.

"That's too bad."

"And you know what," I said, "now I'm kind of sorry you're leaving. That this is your last day here."

"Well now," he said, "that's sweet."

And I *was* sorry too, sorry for myself. I wished that he had another tattoo that still needed to be removed. But there was nothing I could do about his going, so I went off myself, to sit in the sun and be lonely all over again.

But in the evening he came to find me and asked me if I would like to take one last walk together. I was so sad that I almost said no, but of course I went, and just about the time it started to get dark, there we were again, on that concrete bench in the garden, talking about skin.

"My problem," he said, "was that I didn't feel the way I looked."

"And my problem," I said, "is that I don't look the way I feel."

"But you look fine," he said. "What's wrong with you?" It was enough to send my nails deep into my flesh.

"Let me show you something," he said, and for a moment I was worried, remembering the last time he said something like that and his pants came down. In front of me and the spotted old ladies too. But that wasn't it, not quite, it was his hand moving up my arm, where my eyes were already focused on my skin, and then moving on my bare leg, where they weren't, moving beneath the cotton shift I had worn for the evening. He was showing me my skin in a new and different way.

"How do you feel now?" he said.

I couldn't answer. Not because I was unable to speak, but because I really didn't know, I had never felt that way before. And then his hands were moving all over me, which I couldn't quite understand either, until I saw that my dress was on the ground, on the grass, and so were we; and then for one moment I looked up, expecting to see the old ladies standing over us, because Owen's pants were off again, and I could feel his bandage; but the ladies weren't there and I saw only the white forms moving at the windows, before I closed my eyes and put my hands on Owen's shoulders, and just listened.

I could hear his breathing, which was deep and steady, and my own, which was coming fast, and I heard the sounds of the traffic beyond the hospital walls and the sounds of windows slamming up and then I heard the bellowing of the nurses, like so many old heifers who were off their feed, the commotion growing and growing until it seemed that we were in the quiet center of it and I could hear Owen saying,

"Don't worry, they can't get to you now, not anymore."

o

I'm packed and ready to go. Nobody seems to know what to make of it. At first the doctors said I couldn't do it, couldn't just leave like this. And they might be right, but then I don't see how they can stop me either.

It's too bad that bastard Dublonsky isn't here.

As for the nurses, they've gone completely nuts; I can hear their shoes suck-sucking at the floor as they rush up and down the halls.

But there's really nothing anyone can do. Everything is settled. And Owen says that if I want, we can even stop by Florida and try to find my mother.

We'll have plenty of time to think about that. It'll take us all day just to get out of the city.

And there will be plenty of time to think about children. Owen has already brought it up, says he only wants two. I'm not so sure. But we'll have all the time in the world to think about that, years of sitting by the pool he has promised me, beneath that big Arizona sun.

I can picture it now. This sailor. That sun. Sparkling blue water. And me, the fishwoman, caught with a smile.

Blood Money

WITH HER ARM on his, they might have been lovers out
window-shopping.

"Let's go in," he said. The woman did not move.

On the outside of the window, in large, faded red lettering
that formed an arc, they could read Pacific Biologics, and
below that, Plasma Donation Center.

"Tell me again it won't hurt," she said.

"You'll hardly feel it," he said.

Across the street, winos with bottles in paper bags lounged
around the subway entrance. The street was wet and slick.
It had rained an hour ago and now it looked like it might
rain again. A dozen blocks ahead, the tall buildings of the
financial district, and above all of them the Transamerica
building, rose up through the mist and haze to loom above
the rest of the city.

"When we're done," he said, "we can get something to
eat. We'll have money. There are lots of good Mexican restau-
rants in this neighborhood."

"I'm not hungry," she said.

"You will be," he said.

The woman stared at the plate-glass window. A gust of
wind rearranged the litter on the street.

o

Inside it was busy and noisy and smelled faintly of disinfectant. Behind a long counter, several girls in white uniforms carefully ignored them. Above, fluorescent lights hung in long, flickering panels from the ceiling. Finally one of the girls stepped forward to the counter with an armful of file folders.

"First time?" she said to neither of them in particular.

"Not for me," said the man, "but it is for her."

"I can talk," said the woman.

The girl dumped the folders on the counter, then stooped to reach under it.

"Please fill this," she said to the woman as she straightened back up, a small paper cup in her hand.

Then the girl turned abruptly to someone else, a new arrival at the counter. The woman turned to the man.

"Urine specimen," he said. "They have to run some tests on you the first time. I had to do it. There's a bathroom back there."

He pointed toward the rear of the building, across a large tiled area that was filled with thirty or forty cots. Men were lying on the cots, and above the head of each something was suspended in the air. For some it was a bottle of perfectly clear fluid, for others a plastic bag full of red blood.

Plastic tubes connected the bottles and bags to the men's arms. They all looked up as the woman clattered on three-inch heels to the bathroom.

o

A dozen metal folding chairs were grouped at the front of the building. In the woman's absence, the man sat on one of them.

Behind the counter where the girls in white worked, he could see the two open cubicles. Inside each cubicle was a small desk, and attached to the wall, a black, dangling blood-pressure cuff.

On the folding chair next to the man sat a curly-headed boy of maybe eighteen wearing a gold earring in his left ear. In front of them stood an old color television, tuned to the two-thirty soap opera.

"Hey man," said the boy during a commercial, "you got a cigarette?"

The man got out two cigarettes. The second one he lit for himself. For several minutes they smoked and silently watched as the soap opera continued. Then the boy said, "That's some sharp lady you got with you, man. The real thing. I've been watching. How come you bring her to a place like this?"

The man looked at the boy and wondered exactly what he meant. Then he followed the boy's eyes to the back of the building, where he saw that the woman had emerged from the bathroom and was coming back toward them, the white cup held precariously out in front of her as though it contained an exact measure of cooking oil that might spill.

"That didn't take long," he said, standing up to meet her.

"It's a small cup," she said. "Now what?"

"Now our fingers," he said.

He led her back to the counter. After a while one of the girls in white came to collect the cup and prick their fingers. When the cold metal punctured the woman's flesh she jerked, but the girl held the finger firmly, as though it were a small tricky animal. The boy with the gold earring winked as the woman's blood rose in a tiny tube.

"That wasn't bad, was it?" said the man a moment later.

"It hurt," she said.

"You need to relax," he said. "Are you hungry?"

"Not even a little bit," said the woman.

They were still standing at the counter when the man with the recently broken nose came in.

"Look, I'm sorry if I'm being bitchy," said the woman.

"I understand," said the man.

"No you don't," she said. "If you did, everything would be easy."

"What do you mean everything?" said the man. "What do you mean easy?"

"What do you mean what do I mean? Everything everything. Forget it." Then suddenly the woman smiled at something distant. "Anyway," she said, "it doesn't matter."

"I want to give," said the man with the broken nose. He stood beside them at the counter now. Like everyone else, he was being ignored by the girls in white. "Hey," he repeated loudly, "you with the file folders and the nice tits. I'm ready to give."

He was too large for the flannel shirt that hung outside his pants. His nose was purple and swollen and looked very painful.

"You gave yesterday," said the girl with the folders.

"Well, I want to give today. What's wrong, ain't I good enough for you today?"

"You can only give twice a week and you can't give two days in a row. You know that. Besides, you're drunk. We can't take your blood if you're drunk. You know that, too."

The drunk made an ugly face to go with his nose. The man and the woman moved down the counter, away from him.

One of the other girls in white looked up from the cubicle where she had been taking a blood pressure. "Shall we call the cops?" she said matter-of-factly.

"Even if we took it, we couldn't use it," said the girl behind the counter.

"Don't give me that. You just don't like my looks today."

"We'd better call," came the voice from the cubicle.

"No cops," said the man with the broken nose. His voice had risen.

"You can come back on Monday. You know the rules."

"Rules," he said. "Who do you people think you are anyway with all your fucking rules – God?" He waved a fist in the air but it didn't look dangerous. Those on the cots in back watched from reclining positions.

The girl in the cubicle dialed a telephone number.

"That's it," he said loudly, "you people think you're God, you really do." But as he spoke he was watching the girl at the phone, and when she began to talk into it, his arm suddenly fell back to his side.

"All right," he said, "to hell with you all. No cops, I'll leave."

"Go quickly," said the girl at the counter.

He backed away. "I just wanted to give, for chrissake. I need the money. You know I need the money." He stumbled against a chair but did not fall. At the door he turned to survey the room. "It ain't right," he said, "how some people treat other people. Just because of their looks." Then he was gone.

o

"I didn't really call the cops," said the girl from the cubicle.

"I wonder how he broke his nose," said the girl at the counter.

Now that the disturbance was over, the man led the woman back to the television, where the two-thirty soap opera was being replaced by the three-o'clock quiz show.

"Look," he said, "you don't have to do it. If you want to leave, we can leave. I'll understand."

A little later, when the woman had not responded, he began to stroke her knuckles.

"What are we doing now?" she said.

"Nothing," he said. "Just waiting."

"Waiting for what?"

"In a minute they'll call us," he said.

The quiz show was just getting under way. The announcer introduced the first contestant and then it was time for a commercial.

"That guy with the broken nose was pathetic," said the woman.

"Down on his luck," said the man. "It happens."

She pulled away her hand and stared at the floor. "This place is disgusting," she said. The floor was littered with cigarette butts and candy wrappers.

"Things could be worse," said the man.

"How?" she said. "How could they be worse?"

"You could be back where you were before we met."

"Where was that?" the woman asked.

"Married," said the man.

She stared at him with narrowed eyes. "At least I didn't have to worry about money," she said.

He turned silently to the television. The quiz show had something to do with providing the correct questions for answers the announcer held up on cards.

"Antwerp," said a card.

"What's a city in Belgium?" said the contestant.

"There's your vacuum cleaner," said the announcer.

"You know," said the man to the woman, "I've never owned a vacuum cleaner."

"I had one," said the woman. "Brand new, but it never worked right."

Just as the man was about to put his hand on her knee, one of the girls in white called them for their examinations.

"What examination?" said the woman.

"It's nothing," said the man.

The girl directed them to the open cubicles and told them to stand on the scales. They were ordinary bathroom scales.

"I've lost weight," said the woman through the wall.

"Is that good or bad?" asked the man.

"I don't know," said the woman.

Another girl in white appeared, carrying a pair of thermometers, and after their temperatures had been taken, their arms were wrapped into the blood-pressure cuffs. Then there were questions.

"Been in good health?"

"Yes."

"Taken any medications in the last...?"

"No."

"Suffered recently from...?"

The questions and answers echoed back and forth between the cubicles for only a minute, then the examinations were over.

The man and woman stepped out. They had passed. In

their hands they held their reward, empty plastic blood bags and coils of clear plastic tubing. They also now had their own personalized file folders.

"I don't know if you know this or not," said one of the girls to the woman, "but if you give eight times in four weeks you get a bonus."

"How wonderful," said the woman.

o

A minute later they were lying next to each other on cots twenty-two and twenty-three, from which they could see a man in white shoes and pants and white lab jacket moving stealthily around the room on rubber soles. He looked like the one who would take their blood.

They kept their heads up. In this part of the building the distraction of the television had been replaced by the drone of a dull FM radio station, a slight improvement.

The woman had removed her shoes and placed them beneath her cot.

"It's not that bad," said the man. "The worst part is the waiting. Here, hold my hand." They stretched their arms toward each other, through the open air between the cots, but they were too far apart to touch.

After a while the man in white came and stood between them. He was smiling.

"You're a couple, aren't you?" he said. His eyes bounced back and forth between them but finally came to rest on the woman. Then he stepped closer to her.

He picked up the folder on her stomach.

"First time, huh?" he said.

She nodded.

He put the folder back down and began to fool with her plastic bag and tubing. His smile would not go away.

He hung an empty blood bag from a hook at the side of her cot and it immediately fell halfway to the floor in its tubing, out of her view. The rest of it he uncoiled and spread on the cot beside her.

"We don't get many couples," he said.

The loose tubing was in the shape of a Y. One terminal he connected to the empty bag. Another he connected to the bottle of clear fluid that hung from a metal stand above the cot. The third length of tubing he laid across her arm.

"This end is for you," he said.

She made an ugly face.

"For that matter," he said, "we don't get many women." There was a faded pink stain on his lab jacket, near the pocket. "Especially pretty ones." Like his smile, the stain appeared to be permanent.

"What's in the bottle?" she asked.

"Saline," he said. "That's for later."

He began to scrub down the inside of her arm with alcohol.

"The winos like this part," he said.

"Are you a doctor?" she asked.

"Would I be working here if I were?" he said.

"A nurse then? A male nurse?"

"No," he said, "but I took a course."

Now he swabbed down her vein with something yellow that smelled sickly sweet and dried slowly.

"You go to a lot of trouble," she said.

"We like to minimize the risks," he said.

She cringed when he took the plastic-sheathed needle out of his white breast pocket.

"Don't worry," he said, "it's really not that bad."

He removed the needle from its sheath and connected it to the tubing over her arm.

"Everyone keeps saying that," said the woman, "but you know it's exactly as bad as I think it is."

"If you don't want me to," said the man in white, "I won't do it." He was already poised over her vein with the needle.

"Just don't tell me it's not that bad," she said.

He did it. Her blood curved up through the tube, traveled across the cot in an arc, and disappeared down toward the floor.

"Pump," said the man in white.

"What?" Her eyes were closed now.

"Pump your fist. It makes the blood go faster."

She pumped her fist and the man in white placed a large X of adhesive tape over the needle, securing it firmly into the crook of her arm.

"I'm starved," said the man from cot twenty-three after his arm too had been punctured and the man in white had disappeared. "How about you? Hungry yet at all?"

"No," she said. "I feel like my stomach is full of ice."

"You'll feel better when you get your blood back," he said. "They just take the plasma, you know."

o

The man in white came and went several times, made adjustments, bounced between them on his rubber soles. But the last time he came he took away their blood, one bloated plastic bag in each hand.

"Getting my blood back isn't the answer," she said.

The man wasn't sure what she was talking about. "What's the question?" he asked.

"I don't know. I just know I didn't come all the way out here to do this with you."

The man had been staring at the ceiling. Now he turned his head so that he faced her.

"Look," he said, "I can see you're unhappy. This isn't exactly my idea of a good time either. But talking about it doesn't make it any better."

"How would you know?" she said.

"What do you mean?"

"I mean we never talk."

"We're talking now," he said.

"No we're not," she said.

The man went back to staring at the ceiling. The silence between them was modified by the FM radio music. All the songs sounded the same.

After a moment he said, "You don't have to keep pumping. That's just to help force the blood out. You're getting saline now. You don't have to do anything."

The woman looked up. Above her, clear fluid was slowly dripping from the bottle into the tube that fed her vein. She stopped pumping her fist. She closed her eyes. They were both quiet. After a short time the man was no longer sure the woman was still awake.

Then the man in white returned and again stood between them.

"Well," he said triumphantly, "here it is."

In his hands he held their blood. The bags seemed smaller and darker than when they went away.

"You're such nice people," he said, "that I ran yours through first, ahead of the others. I'm not supposed to do that."

The woman opened and closed her eyes. "Thanks a lot," she said.

"No problem, though I can't promise to do it for you every time."

He hooked her bag of blood on the metal stand above her cot, in tandem with the bottle of saline, and again adjusted the plastic tubing.

"By the way," he said, "you have excellent blood. Not like the thin stuff a lot of these people come in with." He twisted a plastic valve and it began to flow.

It was hard to tell now whether the blood was red or blue as it made its slow way back down the tube, replacing saline, toward her arm. The woman stared at it fixedly as the man in white moved over to cot twenty-three, repeated the procedure on her companion, and left.

The man on the cot breathed deeply. Then he said, "It won't be long now. It goes back in a lot faster than it comes out. I don't know why."

"Then we're done?" asked the woman.

"Yeah. Then we collect our money."

o

When the plate-glass window of Pacific Biologics suddenly

shattered, crashing loudly into small pieces on the floor, the woman was not the only one to scream. But she was the only one who tried to sit up. Her movement forced the needle deep into her arm. She screamed again with the new, abrupt pain.

"Be careful," said the man on cot twenty-three, "lie back down. Don't move."

She did not lie back down. She tore frantically at the plastic tubing and the adhesive tape that formed the X on her bleeding arm.

The bottle of saline above her head swayed on its hook and, with one of her furious tugs, smashed to the floor. No one seemed to notice.

The needle flew – sprang really – from her arm. Blood sprayed over her blouse and face. She got off the cot and stood uneasily on the floor. She did not reach for her shoes. She paid no attention to her blood.

"Don't worry," said the man, removing the tape from his own arm and withdrawing the needle as quickly and as safely as he could. "Just hold on. It'll be all right, I'll help you."

She was bleeding badly. Blood ran from her arm down to her hand and dripped from her fingers. She did not seem to notice.

"I don't want your help," she said. Her voice was unbearably calm. "This is my mess, I'll take care of it myself." Then she started away from the cot.

"Wait," he said, standing now himself, "you don't know what's happened. You don't know what's out there."

"I don't care what's out there," said the woman.

Everyone at the front of the building had moved away from the broken window. The empty wine bottle that had done the damage lay curiously intact on the floor. The curtains swayed back and forth in the breeze, and outside it had again started to rain.

The girls in white behind the counter spoke loudly and excitedly, while new donors spoke in nervous whispers; but everyone was for a moment silent as the barefooted woman with the blood-smeared face and dripping fingers made her way to the door.

Across the street, the man with the broken nose was being wrestled into the back of a police car. When he saw the woman emerging from Pacific Biologics, he raised his fist in the air.

"Hey!" he shouted. "You!"

The lights turning on top of the police car, one blue and one red, made slick, alternating reflections on the wet pavement.

"Hey!" yelled the drunk. "Did you give? Did you get to give? Hey!"

The woman started down the street.

"Wait," said the man who had followed her out of the building. "You're okay. Everything's all right. Wait."

She did not wait. He caught up to her at the first intersection, where he tried to stop her from crossing against the light, but she broke from his hold.

"Hey!" he called out to her through the traffic. "If you would just hold on one minute, we could talk about this."

She did not hold on. She did not look back.

"Wait," he said, though he was no longer shouting, no longer speaking to anyone but himself as he stared at the diluted splattering of her blood on the sidewalk. "What about your money? What about that?"

She began to run, a slow jog into the soft rain.

Paco and I at Sea

But what are they looking for, our souls that travel
on decks of ships out-worn, crowded together with
sallow-faced women and crying babies,
unable to distract themselves with the flying fish
or the stars to which the mastheads point:
rubbed out by gramophone records,
involved unwillingly in aimless pilgrimages,
murmuring broken thoughts from foreign languages?

— George Seferis,
from "Mythistorema, 8"

A SHORT DISTANCE down the deck a young woman stands
at the rail. Like me, she is watching the sky slowly change,
the orange sun that will soon touch the sea.

Now and then she glances over at me. I know this because
now and then I glance at her too, and what my study has
revealed so far is that she is not beautiful. At the moment
the sky is peaceful, yet she wears a yellow slicker and hat,
the kind that can be tied under the chin. It does not flatter
her, this costume.

Her hands grip the rail tightly.

o

Mostly it has been smooth sailing. But this time of year,
with the summer well gone, each day brings some change

in the temperature, the sky, the wind.

You can read the weather in the faces of the men who work this ship, the *Aurelia*, just as you can with any sailor at sea. If you are up early in the morning to watch and they are at their stations on time, you might worry. If they are nervous and quick to do their jobs, you have reason to be anxious.

We have had some high seas, but none rough. Mostly the skies have been clear. The voyage has been enjoyable, the food excellent, and these days at sea I have gotten more sleep than is my custom — although I am still up every morning before it is light. I have felt relaxed, and even if I have not yet found a place to land, as Paco expects of me, it has been pleasant to put soil and pavement behind.

o

The sun has set and the woman is no longer here. She passed me in leaving and smiled. I smiled back. Her eyes proved brown and very large, her complexion dark, and I saw that she was older than I first thought, perhaps thirty-five, and prettier. She looked Jewish. And the quiet message on her face, behind the coded smile, was easy enough to read.

o

Paco. He is the one I must thank for these pleasant days and nights at sea.

I met him in a café in Córdoba where I had gone to hear some popular singer whose name I have already forgotten. I was standing at the bar, drinking cheap brandy, unwilling to leave though the singer himself had left.

Paco. There was a man standing next to me.

You are alone? he asked when we found ourselves looking at each other.

I'm expecting friends, I lied. At first I didn't want to speak with him. His suit was too expensive, he was too well groomed, he spoke to me too freely. Such men interest me professionally but bore me with their talk of art and business and women. I prefer to study them at a distance.

On holiday?

No.

What then?

I travel in my business, I told him.

I see, he said, and the sad, concerned look that broke over his face redeemed him. Then I will buy you a drink, he said, for the road.

His concern was that my road went no place in particular, and soon we were sitting at a table and he was talking across it to me with a father's concern in his voice. I did not mind.

When I was younger I was like you, Paco told me that first night. Constantly on the move. I could never decide on anything, a place to make my home, a woman, what to do with my life. Now I am fifty, and if my father had not died a rich man I would not have my bank balance to give me pleasure. He patted his breast pocket. How old was I, he wanted to know.

I told him I was twenty-nine.

Listen, he said, filling our glasses and leaning over the table with his words. To discover you are no longer young and have nothing is no good.

o

We drank until the bar closed, then he gave me a ride to the *pension* where I was staying. He told me he was driving to Málaga in a few days, and asked would I like to come. I said I would. It was a magnificent city, he told me. Perhaps I would decide to settle there.

He arranged for me to stay in a hotel run by a friend of his. Like this ship, it was pleasant. And he was right about Málaga. Beautiful beaches and beautiful women and more than enough tourists with full pockets to keep me busy.

I never saw Paco during the day. Like me, he mentioned business but never suggested what it might be. Sometimes he would stop by in the evening and we would go out for a drink. After a month, I told him I was thinking of leaving.

But you have everything here, he said, so many possibilities. Where in the world could you be happier?

I told him I had made up my mind. A look crossed his face as though it were the loss of someone dear we were talking about. And then he began telling me about the *Aurelia*. It was one of two freighters owned by a friend of his and had accommodations for thirty passengers. It would dock in Málaga in a week and he could arrange passage for me. The ship, he told me, had no regular schedule, but wandered wherever its cargo took it.

Perfect, he said, for a fellow like you. You will see many places and choose one of them. Begin a life of real promise.

Paco went with me to the pier, embraced me, and pounded my back. He told me that he himself was leaving Málaga and did not know when he would return.

I wish you luck in your choice, he said to me. The very best of luck. Then he gave me the leather satchel he had carried with him to the pier.

Later, on board, I opened it. It contained five bottles of Five Star Cognac and a note.

Pobrecito, the note said. *Your father is long dead and could leave you nothing. Do not make his mistakes.*

I have since thrown away the note. I have no idea what it meant.

o

There is no moon tonight, so the sea and sky are made of the same black. The gulls, of course, have our lights to follow.

We cannot be too far from the coast — the birds say that — but I know we are following it rather than approaching it. No one on board expects to see land for more than a day.

o

In my cabin, getting ready for dinner, I think about her. She, too, is probably preparing herself — washing her face or brushing her hair, perhaps at this moment veiling her body with a dress. I decide that she is putting on a brown dress, slipping it now over her head, pulling it off her breasts so that now it falls at her knees. I am especially interested in her legs.

As for myself, I wear a tie. It is always the same tie and decorates whatever else I am already wearing. Paco gave me a number of fine silk shirts, made for him by his tailor in Barcelona. But I am very hard on them and I know they will not last me long.

What sort of smell should I expect from her? Perfume seems unlikely; she does not seem the type to advertise herself like that. Nor would I expect her to smell musky, of perspiration, as I surely do. Clean, she will probably smell clean, a slight scent of whatever soap she uses. And her breath, I am certain, will be fresh.

Paco wanted to give me money before I left. For toiletries and the like, as he put it. I said no, you have done enough. I do not care to have you support my private habits. I have some money, I will buy my own toothpaste.

I am especially interested in her legs. Through the port window above my bed, I look out into the night and see her dress falling slowly over her thighs, dropping like a curtain, again and again.

o

The *Aurelia* is registered Spanish, but it has no real home. During the war, I am told, guns were put on it and it was used by the Italians. But a freighter is only a freighter and the Italians inevitably lost.

It is old. Its engines wheeze and it has been too many times repaired, refurbished, repainted. Its weariness shows.

The men who work it seem weary, too. They are of uncommon nationalities, many of them, and speak in strange languages. They amuse themselves with cards and liquor and music. They have only one home and they are floating on it.

It is not a small ship. There are five levels below my cabin and two above, not counting the observation decks and pilothouse. It is easy enough to get lost. But most of the *Aurelia's* space is taken up with the cargo that fills its huge belly. Into the vast holds I have seen lowered crates of oranges, bellowing cattle, drums of olive oil. Out of them have come carpets, leaking bags of grain, wine.

My first day aboard I met the captain, a sour-faced man who nonetheless shook my hand warmly. He knew Paco. We spoke of Málaga. I have not seen him since and sometimes wonder if he is still with us.

We have already made many stops. From the deck and through my port window I have watched the cities grow, then disappear in our wake. 'Annaba. Iráklion. Cagliari. İzmir. I have walked through the dusty, crowded streets, talked with the people, occasionally ventured into the countryside. But always I have made the ship's call.

o

In the dining salon I sit across from a middle-aged couple who must tell me how good it was to visit their son in Marseilles. He is doing so well, an importer of sporting goods. He is about my age, they note, then want to know where I am going. I ask instead if they have seen the woman who today was wearing a yellow slicker.

No. We haven't.

Waiters fill our glasses with water and set bread on the table. I look around again. Perhaps she does not feel well, I think. She was gripping the deck rail so tightly. Or is it possible I do not recognize her?

I pour myself some wine and offer to do the same for the couple.

Please.

Thank you.

It is nothing.

Now the soup, ladled from a steaming tureen into my bowl. I fear that I am becoming accustomed to this luxury. It is a thick pasta soup, rich with vegetables. I consider its temperature and watch it shift slowly in the bowl.

Excuse me, young man, but is that the woman you mean?

I follow the nod, look toward the double doors. Yes, that is the one. Except she is not wearing brown at all, but a pair of faded dungarees and a heavy sweater. Her black hair just reaches her shoulders. She sees me looking at her. She smiles.

I know she will take the place beside me, so I concentrate on my soup. It is still too hot to eat. When she sits down, I allow the middle-aged couple to greet her first. They launch into talk of their successful son and of beautiful Marseilles – of tennis rackets, the Mediterranean, the coastal village he will soon be moving to. She says she hates tennis, and smiles.

And where are you going? they ask her.

Israel.

It is your homeland?

It will be.

And do you have family there, or friends?

Not really.

Well, they say. We have good friends in both Tel Aviv and Jerusalem. We must give you their addresses.

The mutton is well timed. One waiter asks us in turn which cuts of meat we prefer, while another spoons small white potatoes onto our plates until signaled to stop. Water glasses are refilled. The woman takes a sip of her wine, turns to me.

You don't seem the type to wear a tie, she says.

Why do you say that? I ask.

I don't know.

It is a forward thing to say to someone you don't know.

I'm Lisa. Who are you?

Call me Paco, I say.

Wine spills over the edge of my untouched glass and I spot it with my napkin. I taste the mutton and ask her where she boarded the *Aurelia*.

Brindisi, she says.

What were you doing in Brindisi?

Waiting for the boat, she says.

Her banter excites me, but I keep my head down, purposefully pause before continuing the exchange.

And how did you know it was coming?

It was supposed to be a secret? she says. Her eyes get larger, ask me to laugh.

The waiters seem anxious for us to finish eating. The moment we abandon our silverware, our plates are swept away. For dessert they bring us fruit and cheese. When we have finished with coffee, I ask Lisa if she would care for a drink at the bar.

She would.

o

The night before I boarded the *Aurelia*, Paco and I went out drinking. Málaga was celebrating its patron saint, and the bars, like the streets, were festive and crowded. Paco was in great spirits and was soon entertaining a group of young women with an endless tale about his father.

He was a saint, too, Paco told them, but misguided. One night he came home to my mother with a long sad story of how he had been robbed of a small fortune in an alleyway. My mother cried for him. I cried for him. But later, when the true report came out in the newspapers, he admitted to us that he had foolishly given the money away. He had met a young æronaut, an anarchist, who wanted to bomb the National Palace – from the balloon my father would buy – with a thousand kilos of donkeyshit. But the stench at the airfield gave him away.

The young women laughed and bargained for the right to sit on Paco's lap. One had her hand on my thigh as well. Yet in the end the night came to nothing.

o

In the bar, Lisa drinks brandy and ginger and I drink Irish whiskey. One can see we have settled with each other, know the course and outcome of the evening, are watching it progress with a certainty that the bartender must also feel. She has mentioned a party, later, that one of the sailors has invited her to.

It is pleasant sitting here on this old leather, poking at ice cubes now and then with my finger, tweaking my anticipation. Our conversation has become comfortable and predictable, need hardly be spoken at all.

Why Israel? I ask her.

The usual reasons, she says.

There is a smell about her that I did not expect and cannot quite place. Something like the smell of a field after it has been turned in the spring.

The bar is nearly empty. It is strictly for the use of the passengers; although drinks are very cheap in these untaxed waters, few others are taking advantage of it, and sometimes even the bartender leaves. It seems more like a drawing room than a bar, with glass-enclosed bookshelves, maps and charts on the walls, a large nautical clock between the liquor cabinets.

You were uneasy when I saw you this afternoon, I say. The way you were holding onto the rail.

Just anxious, she says. I want to get started, have something to do. I'm not used to so much empty time.

We'll be in Haifa tomorrow evening.

I know, she says.

It is not yet late, but in a few minutes the bartender will want to close up, turn out the lights. I ask her if she would like one last brandy and ginger. She is drinking them at my suggestion. I have told her that ginger is good for sea stomach and brandy good for the head.

o

Paco told me this about women: there is no point in looking for perfection because to find it would only make you afraid of losing it.

Once, in Málaga, he came to my hotel saying he would take me to dinner. He was with a woman. She had high cheekbones, fiery eyes, wore diamonds at her neck, and when we left his arm was around her waist. During dinner they spoke like lovers, and she plainly cared for him. We danced and drank late, the three of us having an excellent time but Paco having the best, and I thought, yes, Paco, yes.

At my hotel, she waited in the lobby while Paco stumbled with me to my room, the two of us drunk and holding each other up. She is beautiful, he said, and I agreed. A tiger in bed, he whispered. I made some appropriately jealous sound. She would make a good wife, no?

I said yes, I thought she probably would, and offered to make the necessary arrangements for him.

Not for me, he said, for you.

He told me this, too: nothing in the world can hurt a man so much as a woman's truthful words.

Paco was full of platitudes, but he spoke them like a god.

○

On our way to the party, we stop by my cabin and I get out the last bottle of Five Star. She is already a little drunk and holding onto me as the ship sways and rocks. She studies the small, cluttered room.

It looks like you've been on the *Aurelia* forever.

A while.

What do you do with your time? she asks.

Nothing in particular, I say.

Beneath my bed I find two glasses and rinse them out at the sink, dry them with one of Paco's shirts. I suggest a taste of Cognac before we go. She watches me pour.

We don't have to go to the party, she says.

I thought you wanted to, I say, but it's up to you.

She thinks for a moment. Kisses me on the lips. If you don't mind, then, she says. It might be interesting.

I want to tell her no, not really, I have been to these parties before, it will not be interesting.

But I say nothing. It is her last night at sea.

She has lifted her glass, holds it a little unsteadily in the air between us.

How about a toast? she says.

I propose Israel; she suggests the *Aurelia*.

We are being nice to each other. I raise my glass and we drink.

o

It has been a long time now since I have been with a woman, and as we begin our descent down the narrow corridors and ladderways, clinging to each other like the drunken sailors we are becoming, I must admit to myself that I am looking forward to it. It will make the party bearable, knowing that afterwards we will return to my cabin and the curtain will rise on her legs.

My arm is around her waist, beneath the bulky sweater; my hand on the smooth inward curve of flesh that shifts subtly as we walk. And her arm is around me, too, her fingers playing on the silky material of Paco's shirt. I can feel her touch, the sure touch of a woman who knows where she is going even when she is being led.

I know where the sailors' party can be found, though inexactly. The precise place varies from night to night, but always they gather in one of the dormitory cabins at the other end of the ship, deep in the aft, near the boiler and engine rooms.

With our free arms Lisa and I guard ourselves against the tilting walls, more difficult for me because of the bottle of Five Star I am carrying and must also protect. As we make our unsteady way, we are mostly quiet. Now and then one of us smiles at the other, another confidence or another promise. We are on course.

Ahead I hear laughter and I know we are getting close. But the laughter has come from behind a closed door and does not repeat itself—so we continue down the corridor and, at its end, take the last steep ladder down. Below us a rat hurries in our direction, then spins around and rushes away. Lisa sees it and points.

There is so much loose grain in the holds that they cannot be controlled, I explain.

I know them, she says. Rats don't frighten me.

At the bottom of the ladder we hear phonograph music, loud voices, singing. Several cabin doors are open, moving slowly back and forth on their big hinges.

Will you take care of me, she says in a voice that means she will take care of herself, using the words as an excuse to hold onto me a little tighter, to rest her head against my shoulder.

Of course, I say, as I kiss her hair.

○

I am convinced we are on the edge of a storm.

I know there is no reason for alarm; the *Aurelia* is old but solidly built. It is big. There is no danger of it breaking up. But down here, so near the bottom, its pipes are leaking.

○

It is dim in this bottom corridor, only half the hall lamps are lit. We step to the first cabin door and enter.

Inside the cabin it is not much brighter, but I can see easily enough that more men than usual have gathered, fifteen, or perhaps twenty. Some of them are leaning against the walls, some are sitting or lying on the dozen bunks arranged in stacks of three, others sit at a large wooden table in the middle of the room. The table's surface is cluttered with bottles and cans and glasses, a backgammon board, magazines, playing cards. The phonograph music I don't recognize at all. It is full of high flutes and the soft strings of a dulcimer weaving through the talk, various languages. The room is full of smoke, drifting white smoke that smells of sweet tobacco and hashish, smoke that burns the eyes. And the air is hot.

A few of the men I recognize from other parties or from other parts of the ship. One, an old man I have talked with on deck, greets me from a lower bunk with a nod and an unshaven smile and motions for us to come over. But Lisa is already talking with a young sailor at the table, probably the one who invited her, and we sit down across from him.

He cannot be more than twenty-five, and from his olive complexion and curly hair, and from the nearly empty bottle of ouzo in front of him, I think he is probably Greek — and probably drunk.

I am Markos, he says, and squints at me.

Lisa puts her hand on my thigh and squeezes lightly as she repeats her name.

Paco, I say. She smiles. The young Greek looks at me suspiciously, although I am sure that my name is the last thing he suspects.

You were alone when I saw you before, he says to her, but with his eyes on me. And now you are with this man Paco.

Yes, she says. She smiles generously at the Greek, but below the table she is again squeezing my thigh and this time it is different.

I do not understand, Markos says.

He does not understand, I think. This sailor does not understand.

What is there to understand? I say aloud, and in the same moment notice the veins standing out on his forehead, the fingers curled tight around his glass.

He is my fiancé, says Lisa.

Fiancé?

We are going to be married, she says. He will be my husband. Her smile is convincing and her hand has relaxed, is again moving on my leg.

Markos's eyes are no longer angry, merely uncertain. But I can see he is not yet defeated. He is a Greek. And he is drunk.

Have a drink, he says, grabbing the bottle by its neck. We will celebrate.

Yes, says Lisa, and accepts a glass of ouzo.

I will stay with my Five Star, I say, and appropriate a small empty jar from among the movie magazines.

We drink without extra words or much ceremony: to marriage, then to women, to children, to our children's children, may they be born in a less troubled world. The sailor's face softens. We drink to the future, to better weather. His eyes become clouded, his voice uneven. The threat subsides. Her hand has risen, is between my legs. I look around the room.

At the other end of the table, a small pipe is being passed back and forth. Near the phonograph player two men are trying to dance, their arms square and locked. On a top bunk, in a dark corner, a young sailor and an old sailor caress each other, fall out of view. The old man across the room who recognized me has gone to sleep.

Where will you marry? mumbles Markos. Jerusalem, she says. She is smiling. And where will you live? Jerusalem also, she says.

His eyes shift to me. What will your profession be? Financier, I say. I invest other people's money.

He is suddenly, violently, on his feet. Dance with me, he yells. Has thrown out his arms. Dance with me. He strikes a pose in front of Lisa.

I don't know how, she says.

I will show you, he cries. You must dance with a Greek before you marry. He jerks her up from the table. They move toward the music, the flutes and the dulcimer.

o

Sometimes I imagine Paco is dead. His note suggested as much.

He often spoke of suicide, although never his own, and admired Seneca, who, like him, was born in Córdoba. But if it is so I do not understand. If Paco is dead by his own hand, why? He was not a morose man, never admitted to despair, slept well, like myself. He was not the sort to believe all those easy words he spent on me.

On the other hand, perhaps I am reading too much into the note. He told me he was leaving Málaga. On the surface the note said only that it was unlikely our paths would cross again. It is easy enough for me to picture him in Barcelona, buying shoes, having his nails done, taking his niece to the cinema.

But the thing that is distasteful to me about it all is that Paco may very well have intended for me to wonder. He was shrewd, sentimental. He wished to be remembered.

o

She is back. Alone. Markos has stopped to talk with a friend. I see him pointing in our direction, laughing.

He's very drunk, she says.

I know.

He said I must make love to a Greek before I marry — so that I will know the right way.

His experience is with whores.

And yours?

The sailor returns to the table, picks up the bottle of ouzo, but it is empty. He lifts the Five Star and tries to pour himself a drink. As much spills to the table as into his glass.

Hey, Paco, she is a good dancer, he says.

Of course, I say.

She will make a good wife, he says.

The ship lunges and he nearly falls. A bottle slides off the table and shatters on the floor. The lights flicker. My old friend groans in his sleep.

Let's sit someplace safer, says Lisa. I look around. One of the bottom bunks is unoccupied. We move to it. Markos has his head in his hands, does not seem to realize we are gone.

My stomach is a little uneasy, she says.

I offer her a sip of Cognac.

Is it a bad storm? she asks.

The first one always seems bad, I say.

What I told the sailor could be true.

What do you mean?

You could come with me to Jerusalem.

I'm not Jewish.

You've just been away, she says, and touches my cheek.

The Greek has his head up and has noticed our absence — finds his feet and is suddenly looming over us. His eyes are sullen and glazed. Why do you leave me? he wants to know.

She is tired, I say, does not feel well.

Her head is on my shoulder. Another sailor has put his arm around Markos, is pulling him away, arguing with him. Their words are loud and rough.

You should get off this ship, Lisa says.

Why? I slip my hand beneath her sweater. Her skin is warm and soft, and it seems to me I have touched her flesh many times before.

Get off this ship, she repeats.

I'll think about it, I say.

Don't think about it, she says. Her hand is between my legs, and from the table I see Markos and his friend leering at us as they argue.

Deliberation is for old men, she says.

I touch her breast, then take it in my hand. Her head falls to my chest. My hand follows the slight weight of her flesh as it rises and falls with her breathing.

I think I'm sick, she says.

It will pass, I say. But I realize that her fingers are suddenly still, her breathing shallow.

We'll go, I say, but it is too late. As I start to lift her head, her mouth opens, and my shirt, Paco's shirt, is suddenly wet. From the blue silk rises the stench of her vomit.

There is nothing to be done.

I hold her head and look around the room. Markos and his friend have settled at the far end of the table, have a new bottle between them, have apparently resolved their dispute. The music is gone, the lights dimmer than before.

I stroke her hair, wait for more sickness, but none comes. She is breathing in gulps. I will have to move her soon.

The ship rhythmically lurches, hesitates, and leans back. Empty cans roll back and forth across the floor. The cabin door bangs heavily at its frame.

I sit her up as best I can, rest her in a corner of wall and bedframe. Still her head falls forward.

This ship, she says.

I take off Paco's shirt. I push back her hair and use what

is dry to wipe off her face, then drop the shirt to the floor. I cannot take off her filthy sweater here.

A fool, she says.

The Five Star is beside me on the bunk. I pick it up and swallow the rest.

Can you walk? I ask.

Jerusalem, she says.

o

I know the rest. I will take her to her cabin, help her off with her sweater and soiled dungarees. I will finally see her legs. I will put her to bed and then go alone to my cabin. I doubt she will get up until it is time for her to leave the *Aurelia*, and I doubt the storm will delay our arrival.

Her head rolls from side to side with the motion of the ship and I lean forward to help her up. I take her hands. She lifts her face and looks at me, looks at me as though she recognizes who I am, who I am not.

Paco? she says. Paco?

And I hear Markos call out: Paco!

But no, I pull her to her feet and I do not answer to anyone. And I am thinking *Dubrovnik, Palermo, Lindos.* I am thinking *Alexandria. Genoa. Corinth.*

Christmas in Calpe

STEVEN STUDIES the homemade Scrabble board, the cardboard letters and cardboard words. The game's over, he's lost again, and he's cold.

He should go to bed.

But no, instead he redarkens his glass with *bodega* wine and leans heavily toward the gassy orange glow of the little space heater. He is listening.

Nick and Sara are in the next room.

Steven breathes in and out slowly. His eyes are fixed on the Scrabble board, but his ears work the night for small sounds; until the thin wall yields an indistinct mumbling of words, the shift of body weight, a long exhalation, and Steven thinks: screwing, they're screwing again, making love now, screwing.

o

Tomorrow is Christmas, this is Christmas Eve, and as Steven listens he is trying to figure things out.

He is studying the Scrabble board for clues.

Nick's last word tonight was *amigo*. Straight to the triple in the corner, straight to the heart, thirty-three points and once again the winner.

"Ah, don't take it so hard, Stevieboy," Nick had laughed deep and throaty; a laugh that Steven, who is taking it hard, now thinks he can hear through the wall.

"It's just a game, buddy."

"I know that."

"You take things too seriously."

"I know that."

"Ya gotta learn to loosen up, pal, to roll with the punches."

"Like you?"

Nick had paused. "At least I sleep at night," he said.

In there screwing, thinks Steven, making love. Before him, in the cold air, his groan condenses; forms a white moist thing he could reach out and touch.

o

Steven doesn't know where to begin. Perhaps, he thinks, it all started a thousand years ago, before he ever came to Spain.

But he has to start someplace, so he pictures his arrival, the dirty, crowded bus that had crept along the Costa Blanca and delivered him to Calpe, the adobe all baked and cracked under the late summer sun, this half-asleep village he could never have imagined from Cleveland. Remembers looking out the window of the stopped bus, peering through the heat and dust rising from the pavement, to see his old friend Nick leaning against a whitewashed wall, black bandanna around his neck, girl around his waist.

She's so small, Steven had thought then, though he knows now that it was mostly Nick's large and lanky frame that made her seem so.

And remembers the big damp kiss she had placed on his cheek when he climbed down from the bus, a kiss he had found sexy and strange as the Spaniards yelled at each other about the luggage and Nick slapped him on the back to say, "Good to see you, Stevieboy, it's been too goddamn long, nearly two years isn't it, these goddamn Spanish buses are always late."

And Sara gave him a big hug to go with the kiss, said, "Any friend of Nicko's…"

Any friend of Nick's what? Steven's eyes wander over the

Scrabble board, looking for the answer — but if it is here it is not in English or Spanish but some other language, it is hidden.

His own last word tonight had been *shift*.

"You blew it," Nick had said.

"What do you mean?"

"Well, if you'd left the F out of *shift* then you would have had room to play your S off of *ball* over there and you'd have gotten twice as many points."

"I didn't see that."

"Nope, too obvious. Know what your problem is, amigo?"

"What?"

"You think too much."

And with that Nick had gone out, played his final word, ended the game and stuck Steven with the Q, ten points to be subtracted from his final score.

o

"What's that?" Steven had asked right away of the gigantic rock which sat massive and alone on the coast, just out in the water and throwing Calpe into shadow.

"Ifach," said Nick.

"The Spaniards call it 'Little Gibraltar' because of its shape," added Sara. "Do you see the resemblance?"

"Reminds me of Prudential Insurance," said Steven.

"Forget insurance," said Nick, "forget America. This is Spain, that's Ifach, and it's a whole new life for you, Stevie-boy. Want to climb it?"

"I don't know. It looks pretty steep."

"About time you started taking some chances, buddyboy."

And so, despite Steven's misgivings, a week after his arrival they had packed a lunch of cold lamb and wine and olives and marched off to the rock — laughed their way to the top, where Nick wrapped a ten-*peseta* coin in his black bandanna and threw it to the sea.

"For you, pal. Now it's all yours. Bought and paid for. How's it feel to be so rich?"

"Nicko, you get so carried away," grinned Sara.

"On top of the world, right, buddy?"

They had watched the bandanna spiral down, a black streamer, Sara laughing and pointing — short hair ruffling in the breeze and a nose so small it made her eyes seem as blue and expansive as the sea itself. Still they had lost sight of it before it reached the water.

Later, outside Enrique's *bodega*, they had looked up to where they had been — Steven nursing the ankle he had managed to sprain on the way down.

"Well, was it worth it?" asked Nick.

Steven thought about it, looked at Sara. It was a risky business, this new life.

"All right," he admitted, "it was worth it."

Nick laughed his laugh. "Good, good. Now we'll start doing some things."

They had gone fishing with the *pescadores*, early morning adventures in small leaky boats; plundered orange groves in broad daylight and been chased by angry farmers; and at night, in spite of the warning signs posted by the *Guardia Civil*, they built fires on the beach.

"They're afraid we might signal a ship loaded with contraband," Sara had whispered in high drama.

"Is it true what they say about jail if we're caught stealing oranges?" asked Steven.

"Ain't this a night," said Nick, "to remember?"

In November it got cold.

o

Steven puts his hands up to the orange glow and thinks of Ifach — covered with clouds, troubled with unseasonable rains, and now, in December, topped with snow.

"*Por primera vez*," Enrique had said. "I tell you it is the first time ever for weather like this."

"Shit," Nick has said a hundred times since the skies first turned foul, "it's bound to get warmer."

But it hasn't. It has just gotten colder.

The three of them had laughed, at first, to find themselves sitting down to eat in their heaviest clothes — Sara in her ridiculously too-large sweater, Nick in his beat-up army jacket, and Steven in his blue nylon Windbreaker that hardly helped at all.

After they had stopped laughing, after a week, Sara had said, "Maybe we should buy one of those little gas space heaters."

Steven agreed.

"Candy-asses," said Nick, "both of you."

"But it's freezing in here," she said. "We can see our breath."

"Just a little chilly, just a little chilly. No space heater and that's final, we got better things to spend our money on."

o

In the afternoons Nick was almost always gone; cooking up a deal, he said, with Enrique.

Steven and Sara had sat at the table, read paperback novels left behind by the tourists, invented crossword puzzles and solved them, talked about his Cleveland and her North Carolina. What they had in common was being cold.

"Nicko can be such a jerk sometimes," said Sara.

Full of sympathy, Steven nodded.

"All he does down there," she said, "is drink and talk with Enrique about the goddamn weather."

Steven looked at her. She was pouting, her lower lip curled out and down like a child's, and he wanted to comfort her. He got up from his chair and went to stand behind her, put his hands on her shoulders.

"Don't be upset," he said, "you're just bored, that's all."

"You're right," she said, "let's *do* something."

"Sure. Okay. What do you want to do?"

"Stevie," she said, "let's go buy a goddamn space heater."

o

They had shopped for it as though they were buying an

engagement ring — considered this and that model, comparing size and price and claims of quality as they went from one hardware store to another.

Over coffee they reached their final decision, then went to purchase the one that cost exactly a thousand *pesetas*.

Triumphantly they carried it home, a trophy, a prize, an award for their boldness. Carried it home and sat it right in the middle of the goddamn table. Lit it. Toasted it with *bodega* wine and waited for Nick.

Who simply laughed and said, "Shit, you two can't even fuck up right; that ain't big enough to warm a doghouse." And was right.

Steven looks at it now, there, across the table. It has begun to sputter and he knows what that means. It means that before long its feeble flame and heat will disappear completely.

Sara had cried at Nick's words, strange to see. Steven had felt sorry for her, angry and humiliated for them both until Nick said, "Oh stop it for chrissake" and she did, stopped crying just like that, like turning off a faucet, then disappeared with him into their bedroom.

And there was no longer anyone for Steven to feel sorry for but himself as he walked through a late afternoon drizzle, through the wet and puddled streets of Calpe.

o

Tomorrow is Christmas, this is Christmas Eve. But there are no gifts, at least not officially, not in front of Nick.

"We got better things to spend our money on," he had said.

"But what's Christmas without presents?" Sara had wanted to know.

"Just another day, just another day."

But none of them could keep from grinning beneath their words, and together Sara and Steven had spent an entire day in search of boots for Nick. Brown, fine-tooled Moroccan, tomorrow morning they will be brought out from their hiding place on the porch. Nick will laugh, call them dumbshits for going to the expense, and the boots will probably be the wrong size.

Steven's gift to Sara is under his bed, a blue shawl he is worried she won't like—tassels, but the nicest one he could find. Knowing that she has something for him.

Steven hopes that whatever it is, whatever she has given him—and it hardly matters what it is since it is the thought that counts—hopes that whatever it is she has not put it under *their* bed.

o

Steven's fist is clenched—against the cold, he wants to think. And he is listening, though there are only street noises now, a car accelerating beyond Enrique's, dogs barking in the distance, a scratchy record-player voice he can't locate.

At times he thinks he can hear the sea, a block away. It is in his ears, rhythmic, sensual. It reminds him of Sara's month-old pledge. To go swimming on Christmas day, no matter how cold.

He has seen her in a bathing suit. Has seen her out of a bathing suit, on her way to the bathroom, the bedroom, scurrying in her nakedness through the cold. Sees her now. Smallish breasts and slender legs, softly athletic, light on her feet and smiling back over shoulder at him, "Oh hi," surprised yet pleased, Steven would like to think, that he has seen her.

"So damn cold," swish. "Bladder of a goddamn goat," swish. Swish.

Disappearing as he blinks.

Friends, they are the best of friends, Nick and Sara and Steven, as unembarrassed as brother and sister about such things, though Steven always wears his pants to the bathroom.

o

Steven is getting a little fat and that bothers him. He has noticed hair in the sink.

He is cold and knows it is more than just the weather.

135

He is miserable sitting here in front of this stupid word game, and he would like to bring his clenched fist down on it, would like to rip up the cardboard field and burn the little paper squares, but he can't.

Sara made it.

Went out and bought colored pencils and spent two afternoons re-creating the Scrabble board from memory.

"Because we need something to do in the evenings, something fun."

And Nick had said, "Jesus Christ, playing around with a bunch of fucking words ain't exactly my idea of a good time."

"It might improve your vocabulary," she said.

"Bullshit," he said.

"See, that's all you know how to say, bullshit."

"I still don't want to play."

"Oh don't be such a jerk," she said.

"Hey now, that's no way to talk."

"You're just being mean to be mean."

"I just don't want to play, I got that right."

"Look," she said, "I went to a lot of trouble."

"Listen," he said, "you're *asking* for a lot of trouble."

They stared hard at each other, their eyes overcast with real anger, and when Sara glanced over at Steven he saw that she was counting on him for support.

Then she said, "Go to hell, Nicko."

And Nick said, "I'm going down to Enrique's," spun away from her, and with his fist put a neat hole in the door before opening it and then closing it: ridiculous.

A minute later Steven got up and moved toward Sara.

Her eyes were damp. He held her in his arms, began to console her, to tell her that everything would be all right, when she started to giggle.

"God, that was funny," she said, hugging him.

"Funny?"

"I hope he broke his goddamn hand."

"Don't worry," said Steven, unaware that his words no longer fit.

"Did you see his face?"

"Don't worry, I'll take care of you."

And they were still standing in the middle of the room, embracing more like lovers than brother and sister, when the door opened and Nick stepped back in.

Steven's arms fell to his sides, Sara stepped back.

Steven needed to say something, but what? It's not what it looks like? It was exactly what it looked like.

He opened his mouth as though to speak anyway, then saw that he didn't have to. Nick's glare had become a grin.

"All right," he said, "you wanna play a little Scrabble, we'll play a little goddamn Scrabble. But I get to add a few rules."

o

Nick had only lost the game once, the first time they played. It took him that long to decide on what rules to add.

Since they were in Spain, Spanish words were okay, right? Since it was just them, dirty words were okay, right? Since they didn't have a dictionary, if you knew you were right you were right, right?

Puta, poontang, spick, it went, and *vino, bunko, kike, bite.*

"My ass," he said. "You can bite my ass if I ever lose at this game again."

It only came close to happening once, the time that Steven played *sanitize* off the T in Sara's *ballet*, scoring not only a double triple-word score along the bottom, but a bonus fifty points as well for using all his letters.

"Big fucking deal," said Nick, then accidentally spilled his wine over the board, flooding the neat squared field of words until it was a purple swamp of nonsense.

And apologized, over and over — his attempt at sincerity barely audible through the laughter of outrage, Sara and Steven roaring because it had been clear from the start that if Nick couldn't win he would still find a way not to lose.

"Really, it was an accident. Really, I'm sorry."

"Ya."

"Sure."

"Come on," Nick demanded, "you saw it, Stevieboy."

"Yup."

"Tell Sara it was an accident."

"Sara, it was an accident."

"Balls," said Sara, "now tell me it was on purpose."

"Sara, it was on purpose," said Steven.

"You see, Nicko, there's the truth."

○

Sara had gotten out her colored pencils – and the next afternoon, after Nick had left for Enrique's, she began another board.

Steven stayed beside her, watched, and was confused.

"There was no reason for him to do that last night," she said, "no reason at all."

Frightened by his own feelings, Steven said nothing; had simply watched as Sara meticulously filled in the blue and red squares, leaning over her work like a child. She was a little girl lost in her coloring book, and Steven said nothing because he was lost himself, in thought. To see her as a child made him feel older, but not wise.

And it had been with an older man's patience that he had waited, through the morning and evening rains of December, through more of Nick's antics and Sara's broken smiles; listened to the painful sound of bedsprings, studied Sara's face; watched for further signs of weariness, weakness, unhappiness; waited for a way to tell her that he loved her.

○

Each afternoon they had gone together to the marketplace, the two of them, Steven and Sara. Bought cauliflower and eggplant, green peppers and fat yellow onions, tomatoes that were firm and fleshy, obscenely ripe.

Yet he could say nothing. He could not escape the feeling that Nick, Nicko, walked invisibly with them.

In the cafés Steven and Sara drank coffee from tiny cups, spoke of vegetables and weather and Sara's upcoming Christmas swim. Beneath the tables, their knees touched.

"Sara," he finally said in the Café Nuevo, "I need to talk to you."

"Sure, Stevie, okay, we're talking. What about?"

"About you and me."

"Yes?"

"Well, about Nick."

"Speak of the devil," she said.

And pointed, then waved through the mud-splattered window at Nick, who was making his way in a swagger up the other side of the street.

Steven fell back in his chair, falls back in his chair now, as the unspoken words die at his lips.

Nick saw Sara's wave; made his way slowly and heavily to the café, loaded down as he was with news.

"Well, it's paid off. Enrique and I are going into business together. Cockfights. The tourists next summer will love it, let's have a drink."

o

Steven stares at his empty glass.

Sara and Nick are in the next room and Steven, at the table, is aware that he is drunk — on the cheap *bodega* wine that Nick drags home daily from Enrique's — drunk on the uncertain sounds of the cold wet night, intoxicated by the sad private movie he is watching.

He thinks of Ifach. Sees it from a distance, from a boat, a plane, sees it over his shoulder as he climbs by bus into the even colder mountains.

The small warmth of the space heater will soon be gone. Into his glass he pours the last measure of wine. He is listening.

o

"Why not, you jerk? Tell me just why the hell not," he hears Sara yell, has heard her scream, this morning. It had awakened him, jarred him from a dream. Down an imagined corridor he had heard Nick mumble, something about breakfast, something about a goddamn priest.

Steven sat up involuntarily, could feel sunlight on his face. He waited for Sara to speak again.

"No, you can get your own goddamn breakfast."

Then came Nick's voice, booming now, and menacing. Nick provoked, Nick ready to do battle. Steven heard the word *bitch*, heard it smack on the wall, and when he heard the sound of small feet hitting the floor he realized he was frightened, for Sara, for himself, for any friend of Nick's.

Steven had pulled the blankets tight to his chin and opened wide his eyes, to the morning, and Sara, running naked past his half-open door, her small breasts heaving, face contorted, running to the bathroom where she slammed shut the door and was silent.

"Listen, Mary Magdalene," Nick bellowed after her, "when I want religion I'll go have a solemn drink with Enrique, okay?"

Steven sank back down into bed. Still, he listened.

He heard Nick shuffling around in their bedroom, mumbling, getting dressed maybe. Then he heard Nick stomping around in the front room, the kitchen, opening and closing drawers, loudly shifting things in the icebox, banging the cupboard doors.

Banging on the bathroom door.

"Hey, open up."

"Go to hell."

"There's no food in this house, open up."

"Why?"

"Because I have to piss, goddammit."

"Piss in your hand," Steven heard her say.

"What? What?"

"I said go to hell."

For a moment there was silence and Steven had thought *This is it*, but Nick's words, when they came, were controlled.

"Listen, you want me to break down the door?"

"Think you're man enough?"

"I said I'll break-down-the-goddamn-door."

"I heard you. Go ahead."

Steven waited for the sound of splintering wood. Instead it was Nick's voice that cracked.

"You know what this means?" he said.

"Leave me alone."

"I said do you know what this goddamn means?"

"Sure, it means you're going down to Enrique's."

Steven waited. Instead of leaving, Nick appeared at Steven's door.

"You awake?" he said. "You gotta be awake."

Steven couldn't deny it so he grunted, as semiconsciously as possible.

"Can you imagine that, Stevieboy, she wanted me to go to church. Me! Fucking demanded that I take her to Mass. Let's go get some breakfast."

"Huh?"

"I could *eat* a goddamn priest, I'm so hungry. Let's go."

"Uh, no thanks," said Steven, trying not to betray himself. "I think I'll sleep for a while."

He didn't sleep. After the front door banged shut and it was once again quiet, he listened. Could hear children playing in the wet street, could hear water dripping from the tap in the kitchen, could even hear the buzz of a fat winter fly in the front room – but he could hear nothing from the bathroom.

She must be freezing in there, he thought, and imagined her huddled naked on the toilet seat, too upset to cry, too upset to move. Naked and cold, a child, abandoned here in Spain on the steps of Ifach. The bastard! Beneath the blankets Steven clutched at his pillow, listened.

Until the bathroom door opened and he could hear the soft padding of bare feet in the hall.

He got up. Put on his pants and shirt and a sweater, put on his blue nylon Windbreaker against the cold, and went himself, quietly, to the bathroom.

There was no message there, no evidence of how hard she was taking it.

Steven washed his face and thought of the sea. Thought

of them together, him and Sara, on their way to someplace warmer, on a boat to the Canary Islands. He had heard good things about the Canary Islands.

He saw the two of them, relaxing in deck chairs under a clear blue sky, reading magazines, exchanging smiles, playing friendly Scrabble. It might be weeks before they actually made love.

He went to the kitchen. He would talk to Sara right away, tell her how it was, how it had to be.

But Nick. What would he say when he found them both gone? He would be angry, Steven knew that. It was an ugly business, this new life. The best thing to do, he decided, would be to leave no trace — for them to disappear out over the sea like a pair of gulls.

Steven put his head under the faucet, gulped down two, three, four mouthfuls of water. Stood up and pulled in the belly he had lately begun to worry about. Nick was gone.

Went to her bedroom. Their bedroom. Stood before the closed door for a moment before knocking.

"Come in, Stevie. Don't be so polite."

She was back in bed, their bed. A not very large lump in the blue vastness of the woven spread, her head propped up on two pillows, her eyes dry, a book open but face down on her chest.

"A real prick, isn't he?" she said.

Steven nodded in agreement.

"I mean it wasn't much to ask, to go to church."

"I'll go with you," he said.

"That's nice of you, Stevie, but I guess I don't much care about it now. It was just for fun, the idea of it. Like going swimming. Tomorrow's Christmas. I thought it would be nice."

"You're not going to go swimming either?"

"God no, I'd freeze to death."

Of course she wasn't going swimming, they would be gone. Steven moved closer, thought to pull her from that bed. Instead he sat down on it.

"Sara," he said, "I've been thinking."

"What about, Stevie?"

"You're young."

"Twenty-two. Old enough to know what I'm doing."

"There are a lot of places you haven't been."

"I left home when I was sixteen."

"A lot of things you haven't done."

"They kicked me out, more or less."

"You're too young to let a thing like this get to you."

"Funny thing though, they still send me money."

"You should go someplace else."

Sara became silent, her face expressionless. Steven looked away from her, started to pick up the book she had been reading, but then, not knowing what to do with it, set it back down.

"This is my home now," she said.

"But Nick, he treats you like shit."

"He likes to act tough."

"But the way he talks to you, the things he says. And all that crap about cockfights next summer for the tourists. He'll never get to next summer, don't you see. Some other crazy thing will come up. That's the way he is. He doesn't really care about you, he doesn't care about anyone except himself." Steven paused, waited for her reaction. Then, to fill the silence, because Sara said nothing, he said, "He even cheats at Scrabble."

It was a final indictment. *He even cheats at Scrabble.* He looked at Sara, expecting to find his own exasperation mirrored in her face, but found nothing.

"Stevie," she said, "I don't think you understand."

"About Nick?"

"About me."

"I understand."

"No, you don't. You didn't know me before I met Nick."

"You've got to get away from him."

"I've grown up since then."

"I would go with you."

"There's no place else I want to be."

Steven opened his mouth, to speak one more time, but Sara reached out, put her fingers to his lips.

"Don't say it," she said. "It's better not to say it."

o

Well, was it worth it? he hears Nick say.

Steven sits at the table, a wooden part of it. His glass is empty, the space heater has gone out.

About time you started taking some chances, Stevieboy.

Steven stares at the Scrabble board, his unused Q. He is finally ready for bed. It is too late, too cold, to think about leaving now. There will be tomorrow for that.

Then he remembers that this is Christmas Eve; that tomorrow, when he awakens, it will be Christmas day.

Talma Levy Is Falling

...the foreigner who resides with you shall be to you as
one of your own native born; you shall love him as one of
your own; for you were foreigners in the land of Egypt.

Leviticus 19:33–34

I AM IN THE MUDDY pit, looking up, she is standing at
the edge, reaching out for the bucket, and then she is falling.
For a moment she seems to hang motionless above me, fixed
against the hard blue sky, jet trails crossing behind her. I
can see her face and it does not show fear, her dark eyes do
not accuse me. I turn my head. I step back. She lands at
my feet with little noise, hits the soft earth with a dull slap
that sends mud flying, covers me.

I am standing over her.
She is broken,
I am covered with mud.

o

Jerusalem.
For me the days began outside the walls, just off Haneviim,
the Arab houseboy pounding on my door to awaken me from
too little sleep.
"American, wake up, it is six and one-half."

The hotel was dark and always cold, the stone holding in an unusually damp and chilly autumn, and there were never enough blankets. I put on most of the clothes I owned those mornings: T-shirt, shirt, and sweater, and when I was dressed I rolled a single cigarette for the pocket of my nylon jacket.

The houseboy was my shadow; he would have followed me out into the streets had it not been for Mohammed, his boss, at the bottom of the stairs.

"Mr. Alden, good morning and do you have that which you owe me?"

Mohammed's desk was a final obstacle to the sunlight that slanted in through the open door, reaching coldly across the blue Persian tile of the tiny lobby to fall just short of my feet. I never had the money. Then it was time for Mohammed to smile up at me, a smile that was cool and indecent, and welcome my indebtedness with a slow nod.

"Of course, Mr. Alden, I understand." And: "I know you will pay. Go."

It was like emerging from a cave. Suddenly my feet were making the turn onto sunny Haneviim Street, my white breath whipped the air at my face, and ahead crouched the massive yellow-orange wall of the Old City.

At the end of the street I waited for the steamy traffic, then crossed with the turbaned and yarmulke'd and indeterminate crowd. Together we made our way up the steps, through Damascus Gate, and into the early morning carnival: the barker at the newspaper kiosk calling out the headlines in a dozen languages, deals being struck over watches and razor blades and travelers' checks, cripples and beggars and policemen watching it all from the walls.

The farther I traveled into the Old City, the noisier and more congested it became. The narrow cobbled streets constricted and became covered, smells replaced signs, and across the Via Dolorosa I waited in line with veiled women and Israeli soldiers to buy hot bread. A little farther on, at the fruit market, I would fight to pay for a banana. Everywhere the air was thick with smoke.

My last stop was a confectionery on The Street of the Chain. Unlike the other shops this one was never crowded (who buys candy at a quarter to seven in the morning?). A bell tinkled when I opened the door, and out of the back came a small weary man to raise his hand and say in careful Yiddish-accented English, "I know, you wish to buy from me a Hershey bar."

It cost more than the bread and the banana together, but there was no bargaining here; I paid the old man's price and left without *shalom*, the bell softly tinkling, sun filtering through the cracks between the buildings.

One last turn and I was on the steps leading down to the vast open courtyard cleared by Israeli bulldozers. At the bottom I showed my pass to the guard. It was still too early for all but the most devout, so I made my way alone across the torn and broken soil to the Wailing Wall and, just beyond, my job. In the work shed made of corrugated steel I drank coffee and made my curious sandwich, the chocolate turning to paste if the bread was still hot.

Talma Levy was always the first to greet me. From across the room she nodded, studied my slow ritual, and watched me eat. Her dark eyes never seemed to leave me, but only when I had finished my sandwich did she come over to speak.

"*Boka tov*, Ian Alden. Are you ready for another day?"

It was time for me to smile and smoke my one cigarette. Then I was ready.

Taking off my nylon jacket if it was warm enough, I would go with her and the others out to the pits. For eight hours we dug, slowly making our way along forgotten perimeters, filling rubber buckets with dirt and ash and broken rock. We were digging up ancient Jerusalem, sending it skyward by rope pulley, and each day we were getting a little closer to the buried Temple.

○

I liked Talma, but I was a long time in getting to know her. Her English was halting and guttural. The baggy work clothes that she wore, probably her father's, desexed her.

I met her the first day I came on the dig, was introduced to her and the six or seven others by Moshe, our bearded leader; that day she said nothing, only smiled.

At first I was assigned to work with Chaim, a slender, tight-lipped Israeli a little younger than I, perhaps twenty-five, whose grim face and pious manner never varied. I was put at the bottom of the pit, he at the top, and with little to do between bucketsful of dirt except clean his glasses, his hands otherwise in his pockets, he looked down on me as though the ten or fifteen feet between us had been ordained.

When we stopped for coffee that first day, Chaim asked me where I was from. He had heard of Cincinnati.

"Why did you come to Israel?"

I didn't like the tone of his questions, the arrogance that seemed to fuel them. I told him simply that I had been traveling in Greece and had come to Israel when I needed a winter job.

"Then you are working here only for the money," he said, his narrow eyes turning on me with clear contempt.

There seemed no point in telling him that I too had a personal interest in the Temple and its past, just as I had in the Parthenon and in King Minos's Palace of Knossos, and was no doubt as excited as he about what our work might uncover.

"I was a paratrooper in the Six-Day War," Chaim went on, more to the others standing around than to me. "I fought with my brothers right here in the Old City. When we recovered this ground, I wept."

That ended it. Chaim wasn't digging up the Temple, he was restoring it. We returned to work in cold silence, I at the bottom and he at the top; and day by day, as the tear-soaked earth of Jerusalem rose bucketful by muddy bucketful, the silence between us enlarged. After a week he quit.

It had nothing to do with me, I later learned; he had gone to Tel Aviv for some sort of flight training course. Talma simply replaced him at the top and at first the exchange made little difference to me. Chaim's superior glare became Talma's shy smile, that was all; the buckets went up the same as before. But since we now worked together and there were no bad feelings between us, it was natural enough that we should also begin spending our breaks together, quietly drinking coffee, sitting on the wooden benches under the corrugated steel roof if it was cold, on the steps outside if it was nice. If she brought pastries from home, she shared them with me. If I had chocolate left from the morning, I returned the kindness.

We taught each other the English and Hebrew words for shovel, pick, autumn, mud. We laughed together at the tourists who came to peer into the ground, as though the black dirty holes themselves were of some deep significance. We inevitably asked about the size of each other's families and showed the inevitable photographs; and gradually, through simple questions and the language of gesture, we came to know each other as friends. But still, when four o'clock came, we walked together for only a short distance before I turned off toward Damascus Gate and she left for Jaffa Gate.

At night it rained, a steady drizzle that began at dusk, keeping the respectable off the streets through the evening and putting me to sleep — sometimes with a book open on my chest — before midnight. In November the rain became more fierce, a frigid, penetrating wetness that blew against the windows and worked its way straight into stone. Yet the morning skies were always clear, a fresh, laundered blue, the sun a little farther away than the morning before, but always there, and shining.

Then one afternoon Talma asked me if I would like to come to her house, her parents' house, for dinner. We were cleaning our tools so they wouldn't be clotted with clay the next morning, and Talma was smiling her usual shy smile. I told her I already had plans to go to Ramala with some friends. She said she didn't mean tonight, but sometime. I said sure, of course, sometime.

It got colder. One night, in early December, it snowed. It melted on the ground and the next morning was the same as always; by noon I was down to one shirt, but it reminded me that the worst of winter was yet to come. When Talma again invited me to her house I said I was just getting a bad cold and felt I shouldn't expose anyone.

o

The first time I ever saw her anyplace other than at work was on a Friday afternoon in the middle of December. We had quit at noon as we did each Friday, and I had gone to see a movie in New Jerusalem. It was a rerun of *The Longest Day*, and it had drawn a huge crowd, even through a freezing rain that lashed sideways in the wind. I had arrived late and was stuck outside getting soaked; I didn't see her until I found myself protected by her umbrella.

"Ian Alden, you will be more sick."

She was with three or four friends, from school she said, and as we all huddled together against the rain and wind and cold I was introduced to each of them. They asked me about John Wayne and Robert Mitchum, as though I should know them personally, and then, before the crowd began to push into the theater, Talma asked me once again to come to dinner.

"On *Shabbat*, tomorrow, it is a big meal. It will be good for you."

All of her friends were waiting for me to answer. Please, she said. I was shivering inside my nylon jacket, actually shaking with the cold. All right, I said, I would come. They smiled collectively and Talma happily began to tell me how to get to her house. Inside, on the dry side of the plate glass, I said I had promised to wait for someone; Talma nodded and moved off with her friends.

"Three o'clock, Ian Alden," she called back. "Don't forget."

I waited until they were out of sight, then found an empty seat in the back of the theater where I could be alone and try to lose my chill in the heroics on the screen. But it was gray and cold there too, and I felt that it was not Normandy at all that was being assaulted, but me.

The Israeli audience was excited and tense; when the first German died they cheered wildly. Somehow I fell asleep. When I awoke, the battle was over, the war nearly won. Outside the sun was setting through the rain in the western hills. By the time I got back to the hotel my small lie had become a truth; I was sick.

The next morning I stayed in bed until noon, coughing and dreaming and wrestling about beneath the blankets, thankful it was *Shabbat* and I didn't have to go to work. And I realized that now I really should not go to Talma's house; but when I finally got up I found myself putting on my only clean clothes, and two hours later I was on a number fifteen bus, trying to control my hacking cough with deep breaths, riding through the wide avenues of New Jerusalem, then out into the suburbs.

Talma met me at her door, explained that her mother was not well, had not been well this last year, and that *Shabbat* was always a very quiet day at their house. I was glad for that, feeling light-headed as I did with my own illness.

Inside, the place was a neat clutter of old furniture and things stacked, and the walls were entirely covered with woven blankets of faded design. Other blankets hung where doors should be, and I felt as though I had left my own time, taken a bus not to Kiryat Hayovel but into the City of David, and arrived at a dwelling in the shadow of the ancient Temple. Even the television in the corner, beneath a high pile of magazines, did not disturb the image.

Talma's mother, in a housecoat that seemed to be cut from yet another old blanket, met me in the first room with a faint smile. I took her hand and it was as cold and damp as the weather outside. In the midst of my translated greeting I could not suppress a cough. Talma apologized for me.

Her father was in the next room. It was obvious that he was the one who had prepared the meal that simmered now over yesterday's candles and smelled of cabbage. Even though it was *Shabbat* he was dressed in the work clothes of a laborer, and when we shook I noticed that his large hands were nicked and scarred. His grip was firm, used to tools, but cool. His eyes did not focus on me, but seemed to be looking for my shadow on the wall. He did not smile, had the appearance of a man who did not smile even when he was happy, and as soon as we had acknowledged each other he turned back to the meal.

In the front room Talma and I sat on a sofa and talked quietly, of family and the weather and of work. I told her something of the other digs I had been on, in Greece and in Turkey, even in Egypt. When I coughed I felt as if I were contaminating the air in a sanitarium; I was getting sicker and sicker, and when Talma began to tell me about her brother who fell on the Golan Heights, I couldn't follow what she was saying. I could understand the individual words but I couldn't put them together: what about him? I wanted to say, what about your dead brother? Even as she spoke of him she was smiling and it made no sense, and her dark eyes made me nervous because they didn't blink, seemed completely at peace.

Finally the table was set and a candle brought in. The four of us sat down to eat. Talma's father sang a short prayer, and then for the first time he was looking at me directly. But when he spoke it was to Talma, not me, and in Hebrew. I recognized the question.

"No," she said in English, "he's not."

I looked at her to see how much it meant; her eyes were untroubled.

"It doesn't matter," she reassured me.

Her father didn't look at me again, however, or speak to either of us, but suffered his meal in silence, opening his mouth only for food or to ask that it be passed. And when toward the end of the meal I began to cough and couldn't stop, began to sputter and choke on the stuff rising from my infected lungs, it was with pleasure, I know, that he got up and came around to my chair to thump me once, very hard, on the back. I gasped with the shock of it and was cured.

We finished eating. There was thick coffee in small cups, but Talma and I took ours to the sofa. Her father went back to the kitchen and her mother disappeared; I too was anxious to escape. But I drank the coffee, as Talma talked, and when she asked if I would like to see some photographs, I coughed to cover the groan I felt inside and said sure, but then I really had to go.

She showed me pictures of friends and relatives and of herself at school, pictures of trips she had made to Eilat and the Dead Sea and Masada; one picture, taken of her in uniform the summer before, especially intrigued me.

"Every Israeli must learn to fight," she said, "but I find the clothes of a soldier uncomfortable."

I was hot and cold at the same time; I choked on the last of my coffee. In this and every photograph where I could see her face, I realized, even those taken of her as a child, she was looking out at me with that same expression of understanding and unnatural concern; looking out at me, Ian Alden, as from year to year I took up various positions outside the frame.

I began to wheeze uncontrollably. I told Talma I had to leave. She walked me to the bus stop.

o

The day Talma Levy fell, Chaim had come back to visit the dig.

It was an unusually bright Jerusalem day, the ground soaked and shining from rain the night before, and it was Friday, payday. On Sunday and Monday I had missed work because of my illness, stayed beneath the blankets and sweated it out; now only a lingering soupiness in my lungs and an occasional cough reminded me of my strange visit to Kiryat Hayovel.

I was at the top, adjusting the rope and pulley, when I saw Chaim coming; walking carefully across the raw, bulldozed soil, picking his way through rock piles and heaps of scrap iron as though they were the bones of his ancestors. He was wearing a blue flight jacket and sunglasses, and even at a distance I could see that he was inflated with some new self-importance. When he waved, it was not at me.

I tightened the pulley, double-knotted the rope, and threw a few extra sandbags on the base of the wooden frame before I climbed back down into the ground. The pit Talma and I were excavating had become the deepest at the dig, close to twenty feet, and I didn't want anything slipping above me. It had become the richest, too, the buckets of mud yielding important new finds each day: corroded Byzantine tools, crusty gold coins, and dim etchings on flat rock that brought Moshe and the others running. And behind our mechanical calm, Talma and I were both excited. We were at the center of things, we were our own news; we were inching our way quickly now toward the Temple wall, and the best was clearly yet to come.

I was at the bottom and Chaim, once again, was at the top; talking about his new job at the airport, cleaning his sunglasses and watching the buckets rise as though he were invisibly directing them.

"Well, well," he said in English, plainly for me to hear. "I see we are still employing *goyim* to do the work of Jacob."

I kept my head down, just kept digging, but after a moment I heard Talma talking to him in Hebrew, low and harsh, and I knew that she was defending me and punishing him with her dark eyes and careful words.

I didn't like it; I was a good worker and they all knew it. I didn't need her protection. I wanted to be alone. When she sat down beside me at coffee break, I didn't want to talk. When she offered me a pastry, I said no thanks, give it to one of them over there, give it to Chaim, I don't want it; but she simply dropped it back in its greasy paper sack.

"It's warm enough to sit outside, Ian Alden," she said.

"You go ahead," I said, "I think I'll stay here." I tried to make my face distant and preoccupied, but she didn't move, stayed beside me on the wooden bench. And when I felt her eyes fixed on me I said, "Why don't you talk with Moshe and the others anymore?"

"They do not wish to speak with me," she said.

Suddenly I was aware just how much her English had improved in the time we had known each other and how isolated we had become, as a couple, from the people we worked with. Things besides the weather had been changing, and I hadn't been noticing.

"I'm not sure I understand," I said.

"They think we are lovers," she whispered.

I stared at her: was I supposed to laugh? I studied her face and waited, expecting a smile to break there, but saw instead that they were half right, that there was in fact love to observe.

"Tell them the truth," I said.

"I have."

"And?"

"They prefer the lies."

I looked over at them, all in a tight little group except for Moshe, and I saw that they were talking about us; relating the last month to Chaim, explaining the shadowy betrayal of race.

"Then I'll tell them," I said.

"No, please."

"Why not?"

"Because it doesn't matter." The image of her father flickered before me from across the table; and from across the room Chaim looked at us, his face clearly speaking the sentiment the others had been dressing in silence for a month: pity for Talma, disgust for me.

I stood up, turned away from them all. I went outside, sat on the concrete steps where I looked out over the bulldozed terrain, up toward the Israeli soldiers who stood on top of the Arab buildings beyond the barbed wire with Ouzi machine guns at their hips. Small and unmoving, they did not seem real. I closed my eyes.

"Don't worry about it," I heard Talma say again. She had

followed me, sat beside me now on the steps. "The others are just being bad Jews; do not be concerned."

I did not open my eyes. Her hand was on my knee and I could feel its heat and weight. I could not keep from being concerned: for Talma, for myself, even for the others whose ignorance might be contagious and whose contempt, next year or the year after, might be fatal.

"Hello, Mr. Alden, here are your wages." It was Moshe, standing over me on the steps, come to rescue me with his words. I looked up to thank him but there was only his beard, his heavy Mosaic beard, and the white pay envelope that sailed by my face to land in the mud.

I picked up the wet envelope and opened it. Moshe was gone. Seventy-five *lirot*, enough to hold off Mohammed and eat for a week, but nothing more. I put the bills in my pocket and turned to Talma. "What about you?" I asked. "Why didn't he pay you?"

"I don't work for the money," she said.

I blinked. I had to get away from her, from them all. I told her I was going back to work. She started to follow, but I put up my hand for her to stay, please stay back, and she finally did.

When I got to the pit I immediately backed down the ladder into the hole, slowly, feeling below me for the one broken rung I knew was there. At the bottom my feet sank ankle-deep in the soft earth. It was crazy; on other digs I had worked, when we got to a rainy season we stopped. You can't sift mud. But here it seemed that the two thousand years of waiting had reversed their lesson of patience: we were less than six feet from the Temple wall, but we were in a world of hurry.

In one corner of the pit, stacks of black rubber buckets leaned against the dirt walls, waiting to be filled and sent up. I picked up the sledge hammer and brought it down hard on a large rock, and when I was standing over a pile of rubble I began filling buckets. I filled ten and moved them over beneath the pulley, but no one else had returned to work, so I went back and filled ten more. I was working hard. I was busting up Jerusalem, breaking it down into little pieces, and when ten more buckets were full and hauled through the mud, I again picked up the hammer.

"Be more careful, you will destroy something of value."

It was Chaim, of course, supervising. I looked up. He was not standing next to Talma, who had also returned, but was on the other side of the pit from her, keeping a safe, cold distance.

"Send up the buckets you've already filled," Chaim ordered, and without questioning his authority I left the hammer and went over to the twenty already-filled buckets beneath the pulley. I did not look up. I hooked the handle of the first bucket, made the rope taut, and stepped back out of the shadow cast by the earthen wall. Soon enough, next month or the month after, it would be the shadow of the Temple itself. Then slowly, hand over hand, I strained at the rope as the bucket rose above me, and when I felt the slack, the sudden release of weight, I knew Talma had leaned out to grab the shipment.

I did not look up. I kept my eyes on the ground as I raised one heavy load after another; did not look up, but could feel Talma's dark eyes on me as I worked with the rope, and Chaim's cold stare on the bucket, steering it through the air as though it did not carry rock and mud at all, but a great holy weight of gold and silver.

"You two work so well together," I heard him say, "a real professional team." Talma said nothing, but I could feel her receive the load of the bucket.

Go back, I wanted to yell out from the bottom of the pit, it's not too late. Just go back to them. But I said nothing; there were only a few buckets left. When I had hooked the last one I looked up. Chaim's glasses were brightly opaque in the sunlight, and his teeth were obscenely white.

I started the bucket up and it rose slowly; twenty feet against the soil canvas, the earthen wall, then into the Jerusalem blue sky streaked with jet trails. Up to Talma and

Talma's face. Her face...

○

Then and now I look at her face and see the unrelenting
smile there, and I notice her nostrils, slightly flared, aware
with an animal's instinct of what is happening, what is about
to happen, long before I am. But it is her eyes I study: large
dark eyes that dominate her face, eyes that try to read me
as she watches the bucket rise, appear before her, then stop;
eyes that try to hold me as she leans, reaches out over the
deep pit until her hand has the bucket, she is gripping it
tightly, she has the bucket but her eyes, her eyes are losing
their hold on me as I lose hold of the rope, I have to let go,
and she has only the sudden weight of the bucket, the unex-
pected yank, the pull and jerk of a heavy bucket full of mud,
earth, soil, the load of Jerusalem, her balance is lost, her
eyes blink, and she is falling.
Talma Levy is falling,
I am stepping back.
Chaim is our witness.

○

I did not go to the hospital, afraid of what I might find
there. I quit work at the dig and hung around the hotel,
playing cards and running up a bill with Mohammed, who
was grateful for my company. After a week my daily phone
call to the nurse's station indicated she had been released.
I went to see her at home. At the door her father shook
his head and stared at the floor to show I wasn't welcome;
but Talma's voice, recognizing mine, got me in.
She was resting in the room where before I had heard her
mother moving about behind the blankets; was propped up
with pillows on one of the two beds in that small dark place.
"I am not hurt bad," she said.
She could be dead, I thought.
I had made the bus trip to Kiryat Hayovel feeling strange
and empty, sure that my body was preparing itself for some

emotional assault when I got there. But that afternoon, with the distant sun filtering in through the one small window in Talma's bedroom, I only felt relief.

Her father had followed me into the room and now stood silently behind me, his arms crossed, as though he were his daughter's guard; I wondered where her mother was. I stood at the foot of Talma's bed, and when I found the correct kind of courage I looked into her eyes. They had lost some of their heat but none of their understanding.

"It was my fault," she said. "I was standing too close to the edge. I wasn't looking. Do not blame yourself."

Then she motioned me near and reached into a drawer, and when I was beside her she held out the photograph of herself in uniform. It was already signed, both in Hebrew and in English, evidence that she knew I was coming even when I myself had been unsure. She smiled when I took it and I could tell that the rest of her recovery would not be difficult. It was the last time I saw her.

It is a black-and-white photograph and in it Talma Levy is perhaps seventeen and her hair is cut short. It is a close shot, torso and face in semiprofile, against a background of blurred trees and low rectangular shapes that can only be tents. She is wearing a gray, loose-fitting military blouse with faint stripes, and slung at her shoulder, so that it is forward and center in the frame, is a rifle.

The gun does not succeed in making her look dangerous. She is at ease, an innocent and unaffected smile on her boyish face; it is in her eyes you will find the expression that makes me her prisoner.

Now in the photograph, now as she hangs motionless in the sky, she is looking at me through the years with insufferable forgiveness, unforgivable understanding.

Talma Levy, falling.

Barbecue

DROUGHT, WHY SHOULD it bother him? Living in a farm-house in Ohio didn't make him a goddamn farmer.

Eric stood at the kitchen window, staring out over the dry earth and dying grass; studied the barn, the red and peeling paint. Watched as a dull patch of dust, kicked up by the neighbor's bay, became a part of the dirty late afternoon sky. On the horizon, heat sat visibly on the sick and yellowed fields, corn and alfalfa and beans. Drought.

Eric shook his head. Imagined the sound of it rattling, dry and empty as a gourd; as dry as this Ohio summer; as empty as the desert.

Eric squeezed shut his eyes, pushed his fingers tight to the lids. The desert. Opened his eyes. Now he could see a hundred miles in every direction, could see to the very edge of the earth.

Everywhere it was the same. Everywhere there was sand, and if he squinted he could make out, in the distance, dunes. The dunes were made of the same sand he could feel on the backs of his hands, the back of his neck, the same sand he could taste on his lips and tongue and could hear, fine and gritty, between his teeth.

Like everything else under the sun, the dunes in the dis-tance were absolutely, perfectly and impossibly, white.

o

What was he forgetting? Eric considered the barn, the neighbor's bay; heard dogs barking. And from outside, from in front of the house, he could hear laughter: Tia's silly giggle, almost a whinny, and Molly's low chuckle; the bass and tenor roars of Paul and that man he hadn't yet met, Jonathan. Party noises, Sunday-afternoon-in-Ohio noises, but where in it was his wife, Julia?

"Eric?"

Behind him, she was behind him in the kitchen.

"Eric, darling, what are you doing?"

He thought about it. Remembered the two dead birds in the sink, the knife in his hand. "Fixing the chicken," he said. There was a barbecue grill going out front. "Cutting them up," he said, "getting them ready."

"You're looking out the window, sweetheart. You're just standing there, looking out the window, not doing anything."

Of course she was right. He looked down at the two chickens in the sink, already butchered. The two paper packages of necks, gizzards, and livers. The little pile of shorn chicken fat, the veiny traces of chicken blood here and there on the white porcelain.

"Oh, Eric," she said, "I'm beginning to worry about you." This was not exactly true; she had been worrying about him, and saying so, for months.

Eric shaded his eyes against the brilliant sun. It could make a man go blind, this desert whiteness. "It's Sunday," he said, "no hurry, no rush."

The bay wandered over McAllister's field next door, looking for green grass, which did not exist; this drought, Eric thought, was probably hardest on animals.

"What I mean, sweetheart, is that there are people out there waiting for the drinks you promised them...half an hour ago. Remember?"

"Drinks," he said, then remembered: the three trucks loaded high with blankets from Mauritania, drifting slowly north, toward Morocco. He, Eric, on top of the last truck. From below and in front came the sound of the Arab drivers and their families, laughing and shouting as the trucks were buffeted like wooden boats by the sudden desert winds; and from behind came the sound of the dogs, barking and yapping and howling as they trailed the little convoy like scavenger gulls. From where he was, on top of a thousand blankets, fifteen feet above the white, shifting sand, Eric could see and hear everything. "Drinks," he repeated.

"Yes, darling, drinks. Sunrises. Would you like me to make them?" She was being kind, his wife. "I will."

"No," he said, "I just got distracted, that's all. Couldn't find the goddamn grenadine."

"Above the refrigerator."

"Thanks."

"Tequila's under the sink."

"Right. Look, Julia, I'm sorry. I was thinking about this lousy weather, that's all. This drought. I'm sorry. Go back out, tell them I'll be right there, okay?"

"Of course, but...," she paused to show him an uncertain smile, "please try to join the living. These are our friends, remember?"

He remembered. Tia, Molly, Paul: he wasn't so sure about Jonathan. Julia disappeared. Eric directed himself to the cupboard, found five glasses and filled them with ice; poured tequila, then the orange juice Julia had squeezed fresh that morning, into the glasses; had the five drinks on a tray and was at the front door before he realized he had forgotten to add the grenadine.

Through the screen he could see the others, sitting around the smoking grill, laughing, talking with their hands, making faces. Being at a party. They didn't see him. Eric watched secretly as Molly and Tia, with jeweled hands, adjusted their white veils; watched as the men shifted in their heavy woolen djellabas. Words and laughter, like the dark folds of smoke, rose straight up in the late afternoon sky.

What to do about the drinks? Set them down here, on the piano, and go back for the bottle of grenadine? Or take the whole tray back to the kitchen and fix them there? Indecision became crisis. He set them down, started away, started back; found himself without direction. Found himself staring out the screen door again.

Except this time he was being watched, by Molly. And like a night animal caught in sudden light, he was paralyzed. He still wanted her. It was a problem. Her eyes said nothing, held him with nothing, yet only when crisis became panic was he able to move. He picked up the tray and bolted for the kitchen.

"Eric?"

It was Julia, coming out of the bathroom. His wife.

"Grenadine," he explained.

"Again? Above the…"

"I know, I know. Just go out there. Please. I'm sorry."

She left, blinking, concerned. Eric found the grenadine and poured it into the drinks: thick red syrup settling through orange, slowly, like blood. He understood his wife's concern; he was concerned himself. He had started having dreams. They were always the same. There was nothing to see. In the dream it was pure black night, that or he was blind, and he was only aware of sound. It was always the same. A dog barking, a child crying, and a noise he could only describe as a rush of air, like the sound he imagined a glider pilot must hear.

He picked up the tray and started again for the door. Only the dog was easy to explain. McAllister, his neighbor who owned the bay, also owned dogs; big, lanky hound dogs for hunting coon, and at night the smallest disturbance could touch them off, wake Eric up.

"It's about time," said Molly when he finally kicked open the screen. Eric was careful not to look at her.

"Yeah," laughed Paul, "where'd you have to go for the orange juice, Florida?"

"No, I'll bet Mexico for the tequila," giggled Tia.

Heat rolled off the grill. Eric was suddenly at a party, his party.

"Grenada, for the grenadine," he said.

Jonathan, sitting beside Molly, threw back his head and howled. Who was this man? Eric instantly disliked him; noticed huge circles of dampness spreading from the man's armpits out over his white shirt.

Eric handed out the drinks and in so doing discovered he had forgotten to make one for himself. It didn't matter. He took the only empty lawn chair, on the other side of Molly.

"Jonathan was a monk," she quickly told him, "in California." It was meant to be an introduction, but Eric only nodded, displeased as he was with feeling uncomfortable in his own front yard. "Of course he isn't one any longer," she added.

"That must have been an...unusual experience," said Julia.

"Yes," said Brother Jonathan, "though at the time I thought of it as a job like any other job, with the exception that God was my boss."

"What's on the menu?" asked Paul.

"He was kicked out for writing a book," said Molly.

"Ribs or chicken," said Tia. "You know that when Eric barbecues it's always either ribs or chicken."

"Not actually for the writing," explained Jonathan, "but for allowing it to be printed without the bishop's imprimatur."

"Well, which one," demanded Paul, "ribs...or chicken?"

"What's an im-printer?" asked Tia.

"They were ready to try him for heresy," said Molly. "In this day and age, can you imagine?"

"I wasn't actually kicked out," said Jonathan, "I quit before they got to the trial."

"Chicken," said Eric, "we're having barbecued goddamn chicken, Paul. All right?" From the other side of the fire, Julia's concerned eyes fought to gain and hold his attention, convey some important message. Eric looked away, at the little country cemetery across the road and beyond, out into the desert where he saw...dust, rising in the east, mixing there with the thin atmosphere and the reflection of the sun to form a low-lying, salmon-colored cloud.

"Christ," said Paul, "sorry I asked," and, turning to his own wife, to Tia, "What the hell got into him?" Tia shrugged.

"The weather," said Julia, "he's just concerned about the weather."

Desert distances were deceptive, the cloud could be fifty, seventy-five miles away. There was no way of knowing. But without wind to move it and make it dangerous, there was no reason to be concerned, no reason to be frightened.

"Read in the paper today that this is the worst drought in Ohio since the thirties," said Molly.

"Makes one forty years thirsty," said Jonathan.

As Eric studied the pink cloud over the cemetery, he could feel the sun on the back of his neck. Low now, less than an hour from setting, it burned his skin and transformed the old, weathered headstones across the road into soft, crumbling squares of white.

"Sugar cubes," he said aloud. When the trucks stopped for the night the Arabs would boil water and fix mint tea, pour it into little glasses filled with small, perfectly white sugar cubes.

"Does that mean you're ready for another drink?" Molly asked Jonathan.

"Oh yes," said the ex-monk, "they're delightful."

Delightful? Eric reached automatically for the empty glass, glancing as he did at Julia. Her eyes flushed approval; he was being a host. "Can I service anyone else while I'm up?" he asked, rising. Tia giggled and half-extended her glass.

"But I'll help you," she said, rising too. The look in Tia's dark, round eyes made Eric's mouth go dry. It was clear that she still wanted him. It was a problem.

"No problem," he said. "Only two drinks, I can handle it."

"But what about the chicken?"

"She's right," said Paul, "the coals are just about ready."

Tia didn't wait, was already on her feet and heading for the house. Eric followed. As he passed Julia she reached for his free hand, squeezed it. His wife.

In the kitchen Tia put her arm around Eric's waist and squeezed. "Why don't you come see me anymore?" she asked.

"Busy," he said. Her fingers, playing on his skin beneath his shirt, made him nervous. Morocco was still days away.

"Oh Eric, really! I deserve a better excuse than that."

"Distracted," he said.

He broke away, went to the refrigerator to find the barbecue sauce. It was beside the grenadine.

"I've missed you," she said.

He knew it was true. Occasionally this summer he had missed her too; but as the stifling heat and dryness had risen around him he had missed her less and less.

"I'm sorry," he said.

"Bullshit," said Tia, "if you were really sorry, you'd do something about it."

Eric wasn't sure whether she was pouting now, being playful, or was truly angry. Either way, he wished she would stop. There was nothing he could do about this drought.

"Ever since Julia...," he began, then quickly closed his mouth, knowing that Tia would seize upon it, somehow make him feel even more guilty than he did about something he didn't understand at all. But it was too late; he could already hear and taste the sand between his teeth.

"I know," she said, "that must have been rough. I know how much you both wanted that baby. But Eric, it's just no excuse for the way you've treated me."

Eric thought about it. Of course she was right. He poured the barbecue sauce into a cake pan and went to the sink, looked out once again at the barn, the peeling red paint. The child had been stillborn in Julia's sixth month. Absurdly, unthinkingly, Paul and Tia had sent a dozen roses; Molly had been out of town.

"Look, Tia, I really am sorry. I know I haven't been very nice. Will you forgive me?"

She had moved close to Eric, stood behind him now at the sink. He could feel her small breasts on his back; then her lips, lightly, on his neck. He wished her away, but her pressence was too willful, too full of physical intention.

"Of course I'll forgive you," she whispered, putting her hands on his hips, "as soon as we get a chance to make up." Eric felt his body go rigid; become thick and heavy as a corpse.

"What a pretty picture." It was Julia, his wife, behind them at the kitchen door.

Tia was slow to turn around, in fact did not until she had slapped Eric on the behind in a great show of innocent affection.

"I'm jealous," she said to Julia, "I'll bet he's terrific in bed."

"Yes, when he's awake," said Julia. "Now what about poor Jonathan's drink?"

"Forty years thirsty, he can wait another five minutes," said Eric. "No hurry, no rush."

"No reason to wait," said Julia, "I'll get it now. I'll get them all. The others are dry too."

She held up the additional glasses she had brought in; partly, it seemed to Eric, to reprimand him for his negligence, partly to let him know that her intrusion was legitimate, suspicionless, inconsequential.

Eric bent himself to the chicken, began dipping the pieces into the barbecue sauce. Tia, standing in the middle of the kitchen, picked at the linoleum with her sandal.

"What can I do?" she whined.

"Nothing," said Eric. "Absolutely nothing."

"Missed your chance," said Julia.

Eric buried himself in his task; moving the chicken out of the sink, through the thick red liquid and into a second cake pan. After each movement he licked his index finger. After the truck stopped, and they had their first cups of tea, the Arabs would prepare the meat: large, skewered chunks of lamb suspended over the fire, which exploded with each new load of dripped fat, flames licking hungrily at the meat. Now this, thought Eric, was the standard and the model, the prototype of all barbecues everywhere.

When the sunrises were made, Tia took two of them and

left the kitchen. Eric was grateful for the silence until he became aware of his wife in the center of it.

"Really," Julia said after a moment, "she's such a child." It was not unkindly said, but Eric could hear that it came from the throat, the sound of a hurt animal.

"Well, she *is* young," he said without turning around.

Julia yelped. "Young? She has a fifteen-year-old daughter, Eric, how fucking young is that?"

He didn't answer. He knew that with this, Julia's defensiveness, their little scene was over; but for a moment he allowed his mind to carry on, to picture Tia's body, which showed little evidence of having had not one but three children; her smooth stomach and still-firm breasts, thighs that contracted with a kind of muscular willingness he would more have expected, it was true, of a high school cheerleader. He was glad he was no longer meeting her.

"Are you sure you wouldn't like a drink?" Julia said after a moment; clearly a proposition that she would think no more about it if he wouldn't.

"No," he said. "No thanks, not right now."

Eric stared out the kitchen window.

"It might cheer you up."

Stared out across the brown grass that spread like a worn, faded blanket to McAllister's burnt field of soybeans, and their own small plot beside the barn, where in the spring they had spent two days planting vegetables. Why hadn't he noticed it before?

"The garden is dead," he announced.

"It's been dead for a week," said Julia softly.

"Why didn't you tell me?"

"Oh Eric, I shouldn't have to point something like that out to you."

"Maybe we could have watered it or something."

"No, it never had a chance. If the drought hadn't got it, the bugs or weeds would have. We didn't take care of it, that's all. It doesn't matter."

It did matter, but he wasn't sure how. He let it go. The

sun was huge and red now on the western horizon; as soon
as it touched the sand, the truck would stop. The thought
of it made Eric feel foolish with hunger.

He picked up the pan of chicken and started for the door.
Julia stopped him.

"You'll want these," she said grinning, placing in the tray
a pair of oversized tongs.

"Thanks."

"And Eric…"

"Yeah?"

"You *are* terrific in bed when you're awake. Really."

"Thanks."

Outside it seemed cooler than before. Eric attributed this
to the time of the day and was grateful; used the tongs to
load the chicken onto the grill.

"Looks good," said Paul.

"Looks like rain," said Jonathan.

Eric followed the ex-monk's eyes east, to the sky beyond
the cemetery. True, it was dark, much darker than before,
the color now of spilled wine along the rim of the earth. Dust.

"Rain," said Jonathan, "heaven-sent to end the forty
years."

Eric could feel the movement of blood through the veins
that fed his face. Did it show? "How long," he heard himself
asking Jonathan, "were you a monk?"

"Twelve long but beautiful years."

"Beautiful? In what way were they beautiful?"

"I was in love."

Everyone was interested. Julia, Tia, Molly. "I don't understand," said Eric.

"With God," said Jonathan.

Eric had to look away, had to disengage his eyes and mind
from this man who clearly belonged somewhere else, in some
other time and space; his eyes fell on Molly. What had happened between them? Where had things gone wrong? What
was he forgetting?

"And I'm still in love with God," said Jonathan, opening

wide his arms as though to embrace the low-lying purple cloud.

Molly's face was perfectly clear, held no answers at all. "I don't understand," Eric said without looking at the ex-monk. "Surely you lost your faith when they kicked you out, I mean when they forced you to leave like that."

"No, not at all," he said. "I wasn't betrayed by God. I was betrayed by the church, by men." The way he said *men* forced Eric to visualize cutthroats, smugglers, dark-skinned thieves.

The trucks stopped and the Arabs scuttled out into the desert to gather dry bushes they would pile higher than a man, nearly as high as the blankets that rose above the trucks, then splash with pink gasoline as the dogs, from a distance, watched. In half an hour they would have their bed of hot coals.

Eric checked the chicken. It was doing fine. Jonathan was whispering to Molly as his eyes worked the sky. Julia was talking about the cemetery, saying that the grass there had done the best of any around.

"It makes sense," said Paul.

"For everything a season," intoned Jonathan.

"Actually," said Julia, "it's a lovely little place. Eric and I often take a walk there about this time of day."

"What a nice idea," said Tia. "What an absolutely terrific idea. Why don't we all go over there right now?" She giggled.

"I'd like that," said Jonathan.

"Of course," said Julia, "I'll show you around."

Eric tried to think quickly. Paul, he figured, would go; Paul was Tia's husband, a follower. It was Eric's chance, perhaps his only one, to be alone with Molly.

"Great idea," he said, "wish I could join you. But I'd better stay with the chicken." He let his eyes wander. "And I might need some help. Who else'll stay?" He looked at her, looked at Molly. It seemed to him that she could not possibly refuse, could not deny him this; yet he was surprised when she didn't. In a minute the others got up to leave.

Eric and Molly watched silently as the little band of pilgrims made their way across the road and up the slight grassy incline to the white stones; watched silently and apart from one another, although it seemed to Eric that they were arm in arm and already in the midst of their conversation. What was he forgetting?

They would have tea, each glass with successively less sugar in order to leave their mouths clean for the meat, the lamb. The sun was gone now and they were in bright desert dusk. A slight breeze came up, stirred the fire.

"What I don't understand," said Eric, "is why you suddenly went so cold. Did something happen that you didn't tell me about?"

"Of course not," said Molly, "you know I've always been completely straightforward with you."

"What then?"

"I don't know, I wish I could explain. Maybe it was that you wanted more from me than I had to give."

"I only wanted..."

"That's what I mean."

Eric awkwardly turned the chicken, awkwardly because there was suddenly something wrong with the tongs: they had gotten rusty. The problem, as he saw it now, was that he had been entirely too open about his emotions.

"If there's been a problem," she said, "it's been with me. But I'd still like to be your friend."

"It didn't have anything to do with Julia's..."

"No."

Drought. What was it about drought that upset him so? Living in a farmhouse in Ohio didn't make him a goddamn farmer. It was only weather. It would change eventually, had to; it could rain, change at any moment. Eric looked at Jonathan's cloud and indeed it held promise, he had to admit that.

"You make me feel foolish," he said.

"I know that," said Molly, "and I'm sorry."

"I've become distracted lately," he said.

"Distracted?"

"I forget things. Last week Julia's birthday. This morning I forgot to shave, to sugar my coffee. And I've started having dreams."

"I'm sorry," she said.

"It's not your fault."

"It's not?" she said. "You made it sound like it was, like it was my fault."

"I'm sorry," he said.

It would get dark fast now, and the desert air would cool quickly. And it would become surprisingly damp, as though the shimmering day died with the passing of the sun and fell, cold and wet and heavy, to the sand. The Arabs would lay out plastic sheets to catch the moisture. Eric studied Molly's face. For a moment it seemed she might cry.

"I didn't want it to end like this," she said.

Eric wished he hadn't stopped smoking; he had nothing to do with his hands or mouth.

He watched as Molly's lips parted, as though to speak again, then watched as instead she licked them. If there were more words, they were not yet formed. He stared at her, saw white, blinked. Nothing but white. He was waiting. What to do? He checked the chicken.

The outer layer of fat on the lamb was black, charred. The pink meat inside would be nearly done.... He hated the waiting.

If there were more words, they were buried deep in Molly's throat. Eric wiped his forehead, rubbed at the dust and dirt and sweat that had gathered there above his eyes. The others, he saw, had started back from the cemetery. The cloud behind them had grown, now filled the eastern sky. It was almost windy.

"It's sad," Molly said suddenly, "that we're both so sorry."

Of course she was right, he saw that now; saw that it was going to rain. Farmers all over Ohio would be pleased. Jonathan, across the road, waved. The Arabs around the fire laughed. Eric looked at Molly, saw that her eyes were perfectly dry, saw that the only fire that burned behind them was one of relief, and so he went without words into the house.

What was he forgetting? Why, exactly, had he come on this trip in the first place? There was nothing waiting for him in Morocco. Molly had never promised more than she gave.

He stood at the window in the kitchen and stared out at the bay, the dark silhouette against the dying light of the western sky. He had nearly wept when the doctors told him the child was dead; had stood in the waiting room at the hospital, and later at Julia's bedside, and wiped with his hands at eyes he imagined to be wet. She had been more philosophical about it, had spoken calmly, matter-of-factly of their bad luck.

"Eric, the chicken is burning." It was Julia, here, standing calmly at the door.

He rushed back outside. It wasn't exactly true; the chicken was crisp, but it wasn't burnt. Tia was giggling, he couldn't imagine why. Molly was gone, probably to the bathroom. Eric turned to his wife.

"Everything's under control," he said. He felt different. "Everything's going to be just fine now, why don't you go in and get the potato salad and the plates."

"I think we'd better eat in the house," she said, "it looks like rain. Besides, it's almost dark."

He thought about it. "No," he said, "we're going to eat out here, the way we planned." They could use the yard light. He wouldn't allow it to rain. It was time for something to turn out the way he had planned. The others settled slowly, tentatively, back into their lawn chairs.

Eric began removing the chicken from the grill with the tongs. He felt better now. The chicken was just the way he liked it, barbecued chicken was supposed to be a little burnt.

The thing to do now was to revive the party, get some lively conversation going. The Arabs, it seemed, never stopped laughing. Eric wished he could understand their language, could interpret what was so incessantly funny; he watched as the charred lamb was pulled from the fire. Even this they found hysterical.

"Well, how was the cemetery?"

"Dead," said Paul. No one bothered to laugh.

"Interesting," said Tia. "All those old tombstones. I even found one with my last name on it, *Pedersen, Died 1876*. My age, too. Some coincidence, huh?" She managed to glare at Eric through her smile. "Wonder what she died of."

"Premature senility," suggested Paul. Her husband.

"Oh no, a broken heart I'm sure," said Jonathan. "They just didn't want to say so on the stone."

It was the wrong conversation. The chicken was off the grill, on a tray, ready to be served as soon as Julia returned from the kitchen. Entirely the wrong conversation, Eric would have to change it.

He studied the ex-monk, small eyes set too far back in a meaty face. There was something unsavory about him, something disreputable; something that made the man sweat hard even when the sun had set and the temperature had dropped.

"Jonathan?" he said. Eric felt strong.

"Yes?" said the ex-monk.

"I've been wondering...meaning to ask you...don't know why I didn't ask you before..."

"Yes?"

"What was your book about? The one they kicked you out of the monastery for?"

Rain, drought, dust, for a moment none of it mattered. Eric settled comfortably into his chair. He was going to make things go his way.

"Dogs," said Jonathan.

Dogs? Eric floundered, sat forward before he had fully sat down. "Dogs?"

"There was a strange-looking dog in the cemetery," said Tia. "A big red one."

"What could be so bad about a dog book," asked Eric, "that it could get you excommunicated?"

"Nothing, of course." It was the ex-monk's turn now, and his eyes, like the coals of the fire, seemed to glow in the gathering dark.

"There seemed to be something wrong with him," said Tia.

"It was about breeding," said Molly, announcing her return. There was a note of comic disgust in her voice.

"It was a sort of 'how-to' book," said Jonathan, "for dog-lovers. My abbott found it obscene. My abbott, in the opinion of many, is a very small man."

"Arabs hate dogs," said Eric. He wasn't sure why, wasn't sure why he said it; it had something to do with religion. Something to do with the animal's uncleanliness. But whatever the reason, it didn't prevent the dogs from following the trucks deep into the desert sands; didn't prevent them from coming, in the end, to the fire; didn't stop them from seeking out, when the men had finished serving themselves, whatever food and warmth would not be denied.

"It looked like one of McAllister's hound dogs," said Julia, passing out the plates.

"It was a redbone," said Jonathan, glowing with special knowledge, "a fine breed not yet recognized by the AKC. Sensitive noses, excellent hunters."

"McAllister's dogs are always chained up," said Eric, looking hard at his wife. Trying to put things in order, figure things out. "Remember?"

"I'm just saying what I saw, sweetheart. That's all. Don't be angry."

He wasn't angry, he was remembering. The dogs coming much too close to the fire. Looking for food, finding none. And in their hunger, and confusion, and perhaps for distraction, two of them mating in front of the Arabs.

Eric put his knuckles to his eyes, blinked. It was nearly dark now and the air was thick. Above the cemetery, Jonathan's cloud had risen. Tonight there would be no stars.

And remembers, the boy picking up the shovel, loading it with live coals from the fire.

No stars and very little kindness. What was it that filled

the night air? Eric raised his nose and sniffed. The wind had started to blow. It was the smell of ozone, the stench of change; something he had forgotten?

Remembers, the boy sneaking up behind the coupled dogs, theatrically positioning himself behind them, depositing the shovelful of hot coals over them. The smell was the smell of hot, burning terror.

And Eric remembers the screams, so nearly human, as the dogs – still locked together – returned to the desert, dragging each other in turns, mutually imprisoned by their sex.

The Arabs laughed. Eric turned away; and as his guests gathered with their plates around the grill, around the chicken, he went to the house to turn on the yard light.

As he walked, dust rose at his feet. The wind carried it away to the south. At the house he stood perfectly still, listening to the sound of someone breathing behind him.

"Eric?"

Julia, his wife.

"Yes?"

She put her arm around his waist.

"I was wrong," she said, "the chicken isn't burnt at all. You did beautifully."

"Thanks."

When he touched the switch, the yard light suddenly threw an opalescent arc across the brown grass, a hazy halo of smoke and dust. Eric started back to the grill.

"Wait," she said. "There's something more I want to tell you."

"What?"

"I know...I mean I think I understand what's been bothering you."

"The weather, like I said."

"Don't be silly."

Ozone, the smell of change. "This drought," he said.

"It's going to rain, Eric."

"It doesn't matter."

"What if I said something is different?"

"It wouldn't matter."

"Eric, I'm pregnant again."

He could smell the earth now, the unlocking of the ground. Could taste microscopic particles of moisture on his tongue. It mattered.

When they got to Morocco, when he could clean the sand from his hair and from beneath his nails, they would talk. There would be time then.

Eric looked at her, Julia, his wife; bent forward and kissed her lightly on the lips. A flower, she smiled at him. The Arabs, from the circle of light, waved.

"Is...everything all right?" she asked softly.

"Yes," he said, "it's time to eat."

He took her arm. Together they returned to the others. He used his fingers, rather than the tongs, to place a chicken breast and wing on her plate. She smiled thanks.

"Here comes the rain," said Paul.

"Here comes our friend," said Jonathan, pointing at the big red hound dog that had entered the yard, stood for a moment at the edge of the circle of light, and was now cautiously approaching the grill. Eric could see a broken chain hanging at its neck.

"He just wants something to eat," said Tia.

Of course Julia had been right, they would have to go inside. Not only was it clearly going to rain, the wind had started to gust, and the others were only eyeing their food now, waiting for the official word, waiting for Eric to reverse himself.

"Here boy, here boy," sang Paul, extending toward the uninvited guest a perfectly good chicken leg.

All right, they would go inside. They would start over, he and Julia, put everything behind them and begin again. She was his wife. She was with him. In a few days they would be out of the desert, the laughter of the Arabs would be behind them, everything would be different.

Julia gasped. The sound of it made the blood in Eric's face stop circulating.

"Christ be merciful," said Jonathan; and Eric watched as the ex-monk's hand reached out to inscribe a cross in the thick air.

They all watched as the dog, in the middle of the party now, turned in a slow and painful pivot away from the ex-monk's gesture, away from Tia and Molly, away even from Paul and the chicken leg, to face him: Eric.

Watched as the big red dog took a clumsy step forward, revealing the great flap of raw meat hanging at its flank; took another step and stopped.

The broken chain swung freely at its neck, not quite sweeping the ground, flashing white and silver in the light. The dog's bloodshot eyes were pools of silence.

"Must have been hit by a car," moaned Tia.

"Or gotten in a fight with a badger," said Jonathan. "That's more likely."

"It's in shock," said Paul.

Eric stared at the dog, the wet open mouth, the red hanging tongue. It was not afraid, he could see that; could see that the animal had accepted this thing that had happened and was now only looking for comfort.

Blood dripped to the brown grass.

They would begin again, thought Eric. The dog waited patiently. Eric would wrap its leg in a blanket, lift the animal into the back seat of his car, and the two of them, Eric and Julia, his wife, would take it to the vet. The Arabs would laugh.

Eric lifted his eyes to the night, listened to the wet wind, the cry of a child, the chilly promise of rain; stood before the broken dog and waited for it to bark, just once, to speak to him. To say that everything would be all right.